Hervé Guibert

Suzanne and Louise
(a photo novel)

SUZANNE AND LOUISE
By Hervé Guibert

Originally published as
Suzanne et Louise by
Éditions Libres Haller, 1980
Subsequently published by
Gallimard, 2005 and 2019

This translation published by
Magic Hour Press, 2024

Conceived of and initiated by Philo Cohen
Translated by Christine Pichini
Edited by Nicolas Linnert
Designed by Stoodio Santiago da Silva,
Ana Cecilia Brena
Proofread by Charity Coleman
Lithography by Max-Color, Berlin
Printed in Germany by
Gutenberg Beuys Feindruckerei

Distributed by:

ARTBOOK/DAP
75 Broad Street, Suite 630
New York, NY 10004
Artbook.com

ISBN 978-1-7389013-3-3

www.magichour.press

Hervé Guibert

Suzanne and Louise
(a photo novel)

Magic Hour Press

They Let Down Their Hair
Moyra Davey

I was introduced to Hervé Guibert by two friends, both photographers, who first excitedly pulled up photographs on a screen, and shortly after loaned me a copy of Guibert's essay collection *Ghost Image*.[1] I became a fan, immersed myself in his oeuvre, and soon understood *Suzanne et Louise* as a prized rarity: it is his only monograph where his full gifts as an image maker and as a writer combine. Guibert called *Suzanne et Louise* a "roman-photo," and set the text densely in his own hand. Excepting the exhibition booklet *Le Seul visage,* (itself a small gem) it is also the only photo book published in his lifetime—in 1980, the same year as *Camera Lucida* by his friend Roland Barthes, to whom Guibert seems to nod, over the inscrutable, deathly quality of photos, those shadows that write themselves.

Guibert would often speak of the two practices—writing and photography—in tandem. In *Le Seul visage* he declares that as a writer, he has no scruples because a text is largely about himself, whereas photographs, often of his intimates, simultaneously risk betrayal and bear witness to his love. In his short essay "The Perfect Image," Guibert misses a shot, but reclaims it "on the sensitized surface of memory, to be developed and fixed by writing." And in his diary, he noted: "…it is necessary to surrender to the pure events of writing (just as the most pure photographs are pure events of light)."[2]

Guibert was eighteen when his father loaned him his new Rollei to

1   Pradeep Dalal and Heinz Peter Knes

2   Roland Barthes, interviewed by Jean-Marie Benoist and Bernard-Henri Lévy, "La photographie." *Roland Barthes, fragments de voix - Les Grandes Heures Ina / Radio France.* France Culture, 1977. Paris, Radio France, 2004. Audio CD.

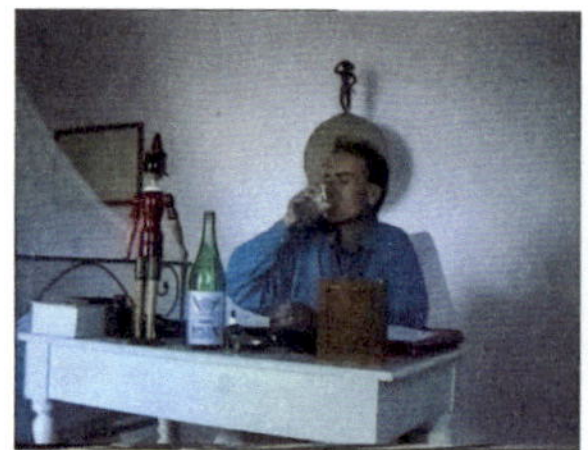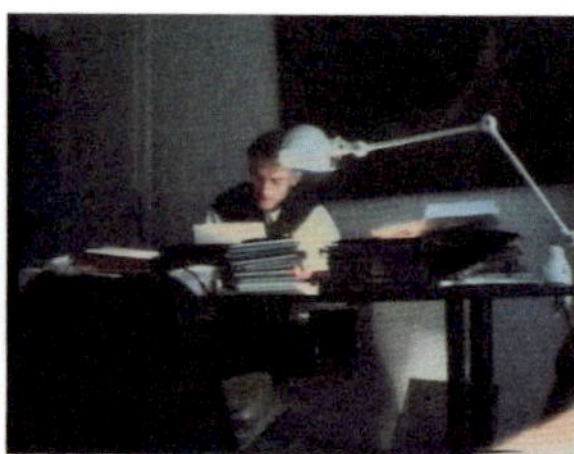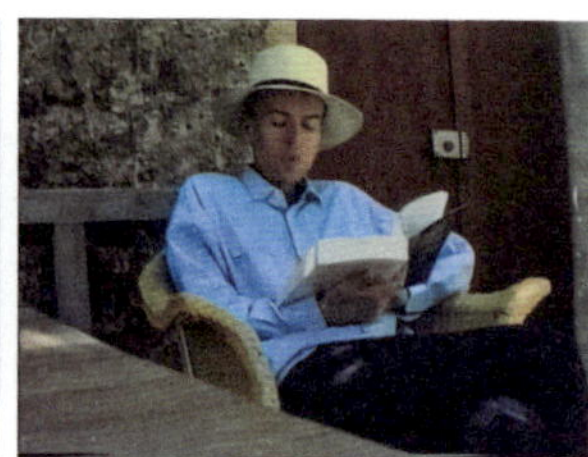

Stills from *La Pudeur ou l'Impudeur*, 1992, directed by Hervé Guibert

make a portrait of his mother. This is the forsaken photo shoot rescued by words in the titular essay of *Ghost Image*. Barely out of his teens, with no formal instruction, Guibert had already perfected photo technique by the time he began *S&L*. He used fast, grainy film and took advantage of the abundant light afforded by French windows. Yet he recognized even then that it was not skill and equipment "that ma[d]e for good photographs." He could not quite put his finger on it, like Barthes, who thought of photography as "outside of language," a tautological object of fascination that precludes analysis. This said, both writers acknowledged that "death and necrophilia had a say in [any theory of the medium]."[3]

3 I'm grateful to Wayne Koestenbaum for highlighting this passage from Hervé Guibert's *Mausoleum of Lovers*. From his article "The Pleasure of the Text: Hervé Guibert's Unbridled Eroticism," *Bookforum*, Summer 2014.

Guibert had wanted to make a film about his great-aunts, but they refused. So he wrote a play about them. Eventually they consented to be photographed and, tacitly, to be written about. The result is this gothic novella in pictures, in which the artist, using subterfuge and epistolary seduction, bewitches his shrewd aunts into compliance. Soon they are jealously competing for his attention: the two women let down their hair and become his collaborators in a dense and twisted drama.

We read at length of Louise's initiation into the Carmelite order, and of Suzanne plucking her out of it eight years later so Louise could work as her maid instead. In this servile hierarchy, they live out their days in a Parisian *hôtel particulier* with spacious rooms and high windows, patrolled by the beloved German Shepherds, Whysky and Amok. We don't see photos of the dogs, but Guibert, ever adept at recovering those missed opportunities for photographs by writing instead, gives elaborate and merciless accounts of each pet's choreographed demise.[4]

Early on we learn the great-aunts have donated their bodies to science. Inspired by her great-nephew's project, Suzanne calls the medical school and arranges for Guibert to accompany her corpse and photograph its embalming. He won't get the chance. A decade later, Guibert, in his mid-thirties, and Suzanne, in her mid-nineties, are both facing mortality on the same timeline. In his 1992 film, *La Pudeur ou l'impudeur*, a chronicle of illness in his final year of life, we listen to him interviewing Louise about suicide, and consoling a very feeble Suzanne on the eve of her 95th birthday. Queried as to what she'd like as a gift, she answers: "To live a little longer." Already in *S&L*, Guibert spoke of his work as life-sustaining; after his AIDS diagnosis this wish would become a mantra.[5]

In the penultimate scene of *La Pudeur*, he's in bed on the phone, ruefully chuckling about the look of hurt and dismay on his father's face at the reading of Suzanne's will, and he ends by speculating that his newly adopted medium of video might be what "forms a link between photography, writing, and cinema." Guibert did not photograph Suzanne's final journey, but a morgue scene had long ago been composed on the page, wholly consistent with his lifelong habit of claiming words as proxy-photographs.

S&L is a triangulation. The accomplices intuit and react to each other in a way that is singular for a trio separated in years by over a half-century— Guibert was barely twenty-five when *S&L* was published. An author and artist who embraced wild, fragmentary experiments, Guibert excelled at straddling the ordinary and the dramatic. There is a long denouement with multiple staged death scenes for Suzanne, a willing and sanguinely fatal character. One of these, a failed shoot, would become an opportunity for him to problem-solve with his confidantes; an exhibition of the photographs would elicit their consternation at a review that spoke of "reverse-pedophilia."

After *S&L* there would be few photographs of the great-aunts, but their eccentricities would become ever more fleshed-out across a series of novels, culminating in a devastatingly authentic portrayal in *The Gangsters,* a book that could serve as a coda to this one. We learn of another will, Suzanne's husband's, in which he leaves her everything, but with the stipulation that another woman, his "whore," be provided for. This nameless woman appears in *S&L* as a shadowy figure, bought back from her pimp in analogy with Louise's repossession from the Carmelites. Guibert's oneiric prose and mordant reportage relish their subjects. His writing would never conform to novelistic conventions, but rather performs in granular, snapshot-like flashes of narrative truth.

---

4   The dogs can be glimpsed on a contact sheet.

5   *Suzanne and Louise* (New York: Magic Hour Press, 2024) p. 107

Hervé Guibert

Suzanne and Louise
(a photo novel)

To my great-aunts,
of course.

Prologue.

Louise and Suzanne, two old ladies, recluses, two sisters. Short, gray-haired, and stooped, unremarkable to anyone who might pass them in the street. Two women who've lived for more than forty years in a *hôtel particulier* in the 15th arrondissement. A garden overgrown in summer, miserable in winter, fenced in by a heavy black metal door. Two women guarded by a dog, a fat German Shepherd, Whysky. A dog bought to guard the money of these two women, a guard dog. This could be a crime scene, but what plays out is only a simulacrum.

Suzanne, the older one, is the one with money. Louise, her sister, the former Carmelite, serves as her humble, tyrannical maid. Suzanne tells tales of stinginess, of remembrance, of suffering. She says: "I've never loved anyone but myself." She also says she's never cried, never known how to smile, that she's never danced. Louise tells tales of drunkenness, asceticism, death. Since the pharmacy was sold, no one comes to see them anymore, except their grand-nephew. He's writing a play about them. When they're alone, they don't speak to each other. Louise, at the dinner table, reads her serials, while Suzanne listens to the "Twenty Million Cash" game show on the radio. They don't speak to each other, except when he comes to see them, every Sunday. They don't ask him a single question about his life or his work, but speak to each other across him. They perform, for him, a dramatization of their relationship. They seduce him; they are jealous. He keeps quiet and listens. They are amazed by the interest he shows in them, flattered, amorous. Suzanne says to him: "If you came to see us in the park, people would think you're my sweetheart." They doubt that he's really writing something about them, so they speak without restraint, almost extravagantly, with nothing to lose.

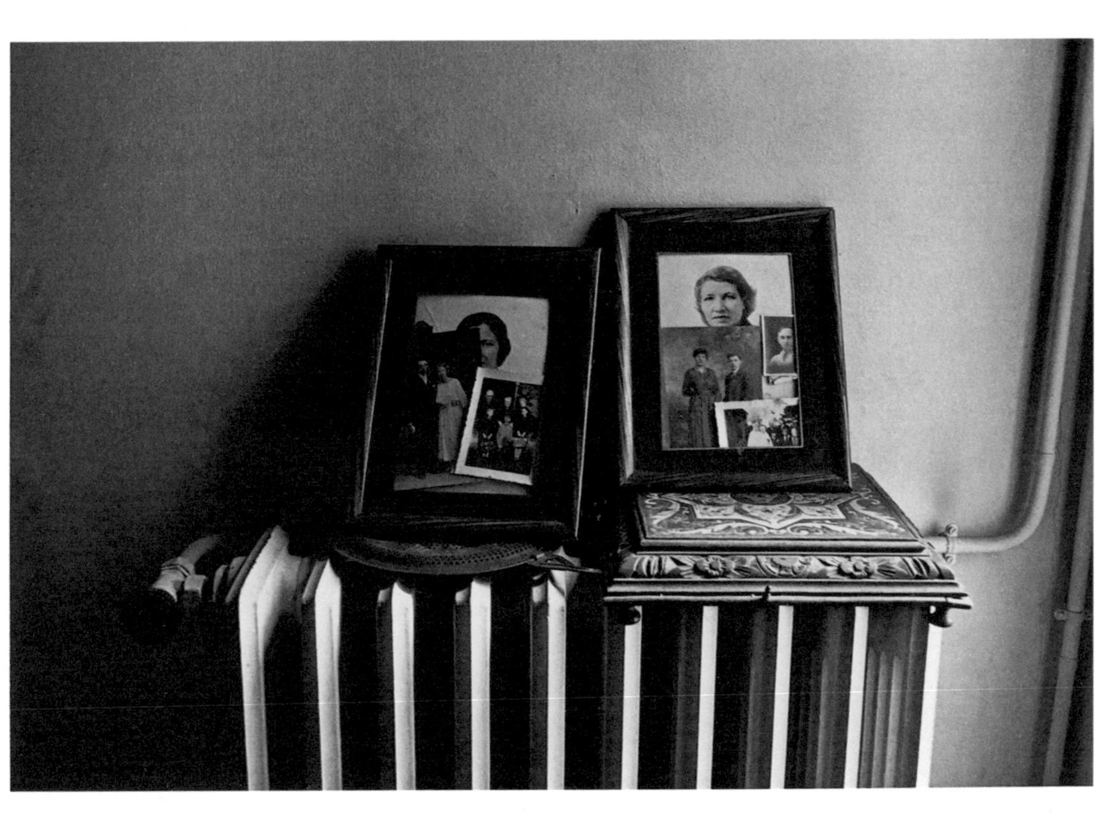

2.

Their life is ordered by a terrible, calculated precision. Nothing must upset their routine. A daily ritual of waking up, breakfast, bath, exercise, then dressing Suzanne, Louise's shopping, lunch, a walk in the park on days when the weather is nice, dinner, then bed. Every night, around six, Louise leaves the house to go to mass. She returns shortly after 7:30 to prepare dinner (a soup and a compote for Suzanne, Camembert and chocolate for herself). It's the only time she escapes the house, apart from the time devoted to errands, every morning.

On Saturdays at noon, it's time for horse steak. Louise eats it raw, not ground, but covered in a layer of powdered sugar. They drink champagne at every meal. They say champagne, but really it's sparkling wine. Louise is in a state of perpetual drunkenness, imperceptible because it is constant. Religious intoxication: Louise attributes a healing episode from childhood to the ingestion of champagne (champagne, miraculous potion).

Louise hasn't cut her hair since she left Carmel, in 1945. Her long, thick, gray locks fall to the small of her back. She is proud of them. She brushes them endlessly, then braids and wraps them around her head. She rinses them with vinegar, her beautiful, gray locks. Obscene for a woman of her age.

Her entire life, Louise gave blood. She regrets that she can no longer give, but plans to donate her entire body to Science. Her body which has never been touched, and which she does not look at, but immerses in boiling-hot bathwater ("Burning herself is her vice," Suzanne says), will be offered up for disembowelment and dismemberment. Suzanne followed her lead, she has also bequeathed her body to the Faculté de Médecine. And they tell each other what will happen to their bodies. They do not know, but they imagine.

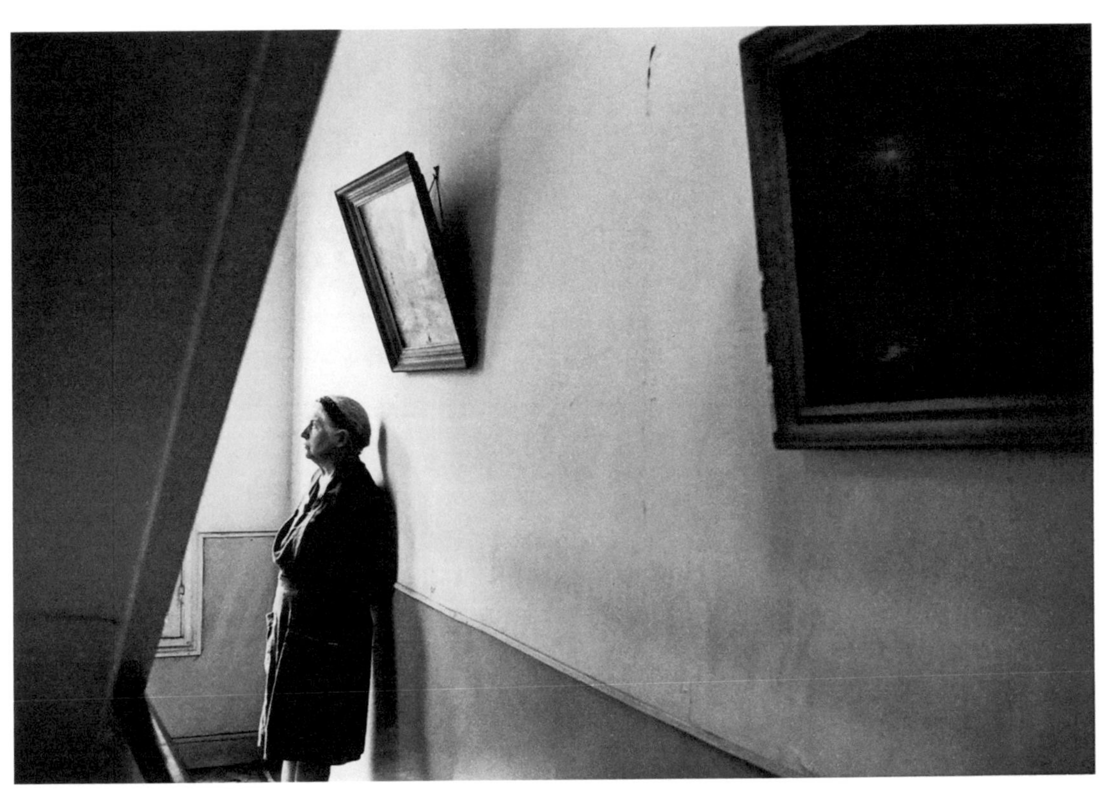

Suzanne takes a certain pride in having risen from the poor, uncultured working-class to her position as the wife of a well-to-do shopkeeper, in having completed her studies and become a musician, after having travelled far and wide, reading Proust and listening to the "great works" of music. Louise respects this accession (her exclusion). "I quit after elementary school," she says. Before entering Carmel, and then working at the pharmacy for her brother-in-law, Louise worked in Rheims for an insurance company. Louise loves frothy things: sparkling wines, sentimental magazines (on her bedside table, *Nous Deux* is next to *Catholic Life*), operetta music.

Ten years separate Louise and Suzanne. They were not raised together. And yet, they share the memory of a poverty-stricken childhood spent in the country, with a railroad switch-man father and a mother from a penniless bourgeois family.

Louise does everything: the cooking, the laundry, the cleaning, the shopping. It's she who dresses and bathes the partially disabled Suzanne. The water she throws on Suzanne's body is always too hot, the food she serves her overcooked and cold. The pair of scissors she uses to clip Suzanne's toenails often cut into her skin.

Not necessarily in "narrative order," some minor events that end up disturbing their daily routine: a bell ringing, a bad dream, the dog dying. Suzanne refuses to take her daily walk for no reason. Louise overhears her talking to herself. Suzanne pays Louise, very little. Louise is her only heir. Louise puts her salary in the collection box during mass. She squanders her money on wine and wishful thinking. No one will ever know why Louise entered Carmel, forty years ago, and why she left, eight years later.

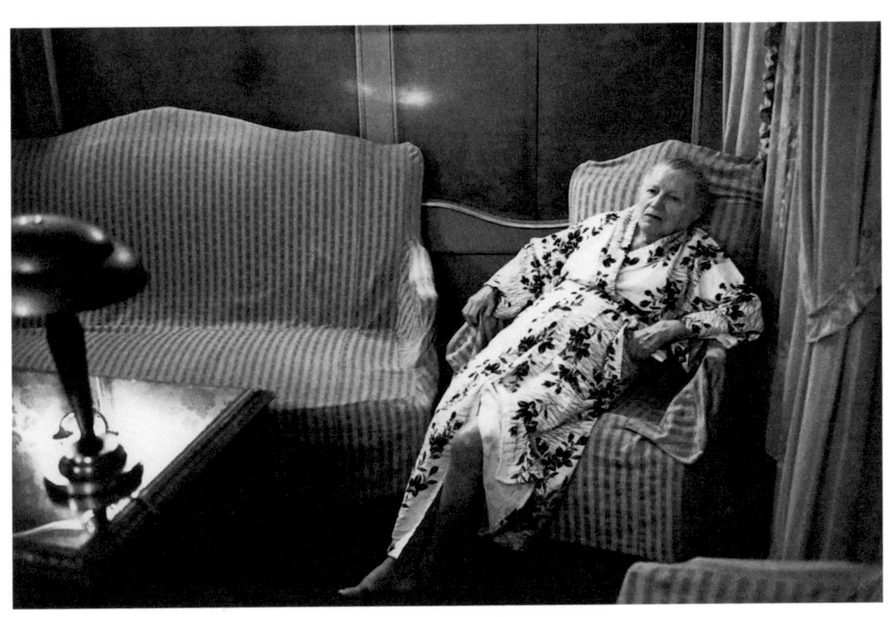

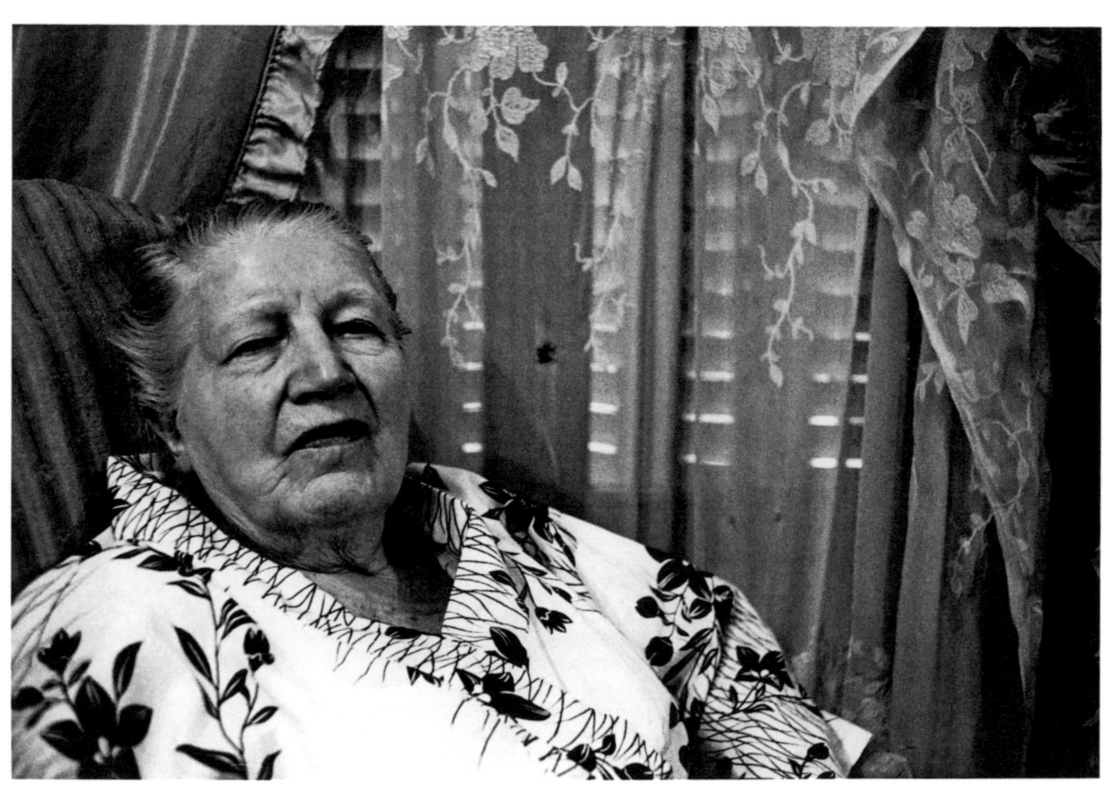

The play.

One Sunday, behind Louise's back, Suzanne says to me, "That play that you wrote about us, I'd really like to read it, after all." She asks me to bring her a copy the following Sunday, and to hide it underneath my blazer when Louise comes to let me in, since she thinks Louise won't appreciate it. When I hand her the stack of stapled photocopies, she immediately hides it, without even looking at it, in a drawer of her bureau, saying, "If I die in the meantime. . ." Suzanne never calls me, out of a concern for saving money, perhaps, or for fear of bothering me; I'm always the one who calls. But that Monday evening, as soon as Louise has left for mass, Suzanne telephones me, and in a trembling but determined voice, says:

"My heart is racing. I already tried calling you last night, but you weren't home. So, listen, you might not be happy about this, but you're going to have to change some things. First of all, our names aren't Louise and Suzanne, our names are Hortense and Patricia. We don't live in a mansion in the 15th arrondissement, we live in an apartment in a modern building, next to the Jardin des Plantes. We didn't used to be pharmacists, we ran an old hardware store. Also, change the dog's name, Whysky is too specific, someone might recognize him. Call him something like Sardanapalus. You say that I took 100 francs from the drawer every day — you must be crazy! — we'll have the taxman after us. And then, that thing about the safe hidden behind a painting, you can't keep that in, someone will come here and torture us until we tell him where it is, regardless of what's inside. . . Take out that bath scene, too, it will hurt Louise's feelings. . . You know, when I say all these things, it's not for me, I don't care, it's for your sake, you know, you're just asking for a defamation suit. . . "

Suzanne's legs.

Today, for the first time, Suzanne allowed me to photograph her legs, at the foot of the sofa that's fitted with a slipcover, she took off her slippers, she lifted her nightgown above her knees and said, "Call the photo, 'Legs of a cripple,'" and I said, "No, it will be called, 'Suzanne's legs.'" "Well, so much for my modesty," she said. Next time, I'll photograph Louise's naked legs and feet, next to that huge bone with red teeth marks that Whysky chews.

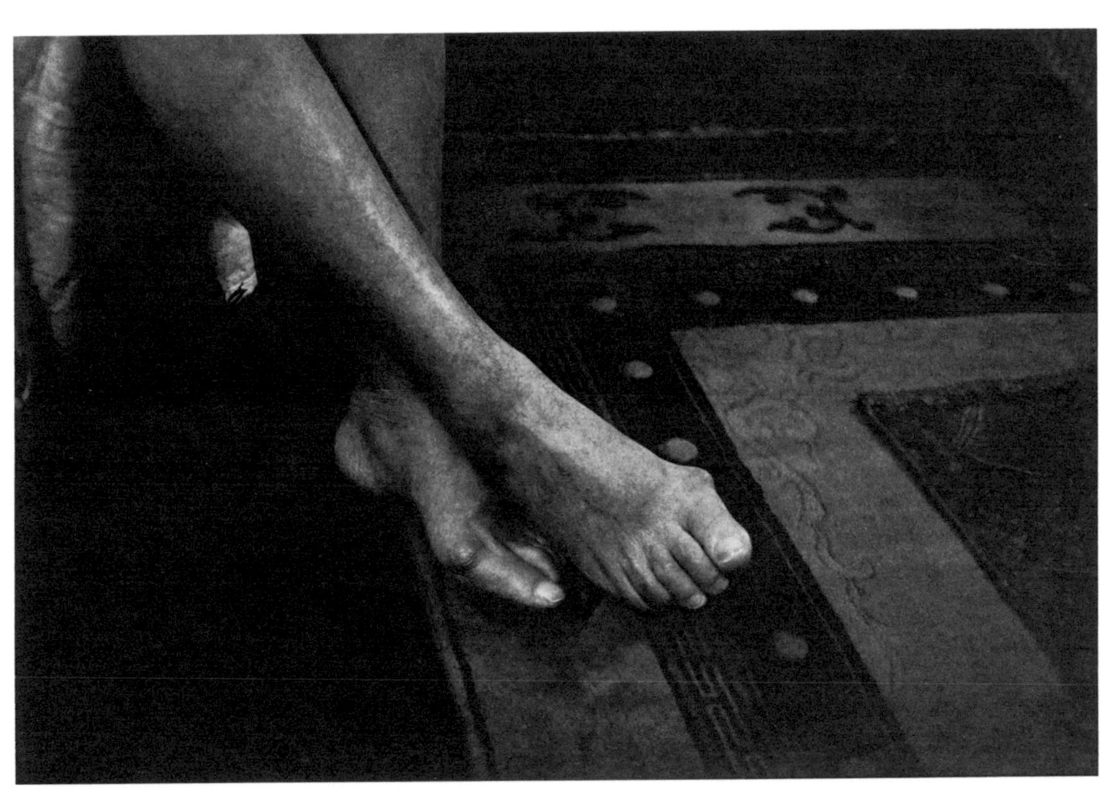

Photography.

I think things other than lenses make "good photos," ethereal things, of the order of love, or of the soul, forces that pass through and inscribe themselves, fatally, as the text that gets written in spite of ourselves, dictated by a higher voice. . .

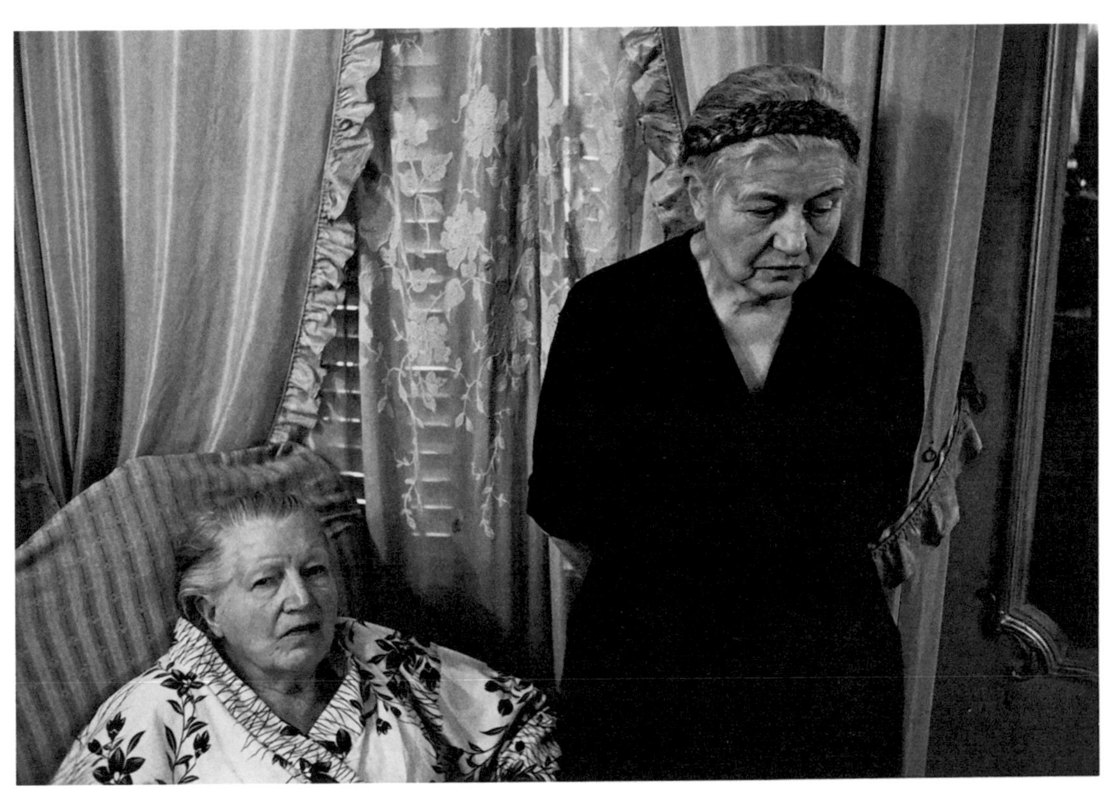

Carmel.

Louise tells me about Carmel, after dinner, sitting at the kitchen table. She allows me to tape-record her. Suzanne has gone downstairs to go to sleep.

"I miss my straw mat. I was so happy on my mat! Just a layer of straw set on two wooden planks. The night I took the habit, the sisters covered it with rose petals. When I left, I wanted to take it with me, but the Superior wouldn't allow it. It would have been a nice souvenir. The only thing I was allowed to take was my scapular. Taking the veil, before the first vows, how beautiful it was! A real wedding, a real wedding dress and a ring, bride of God, Sister of Carmel! The night before, they cropped my hair, the way they crop men's hair. The entire length of the chapel, rows of sisters, their faces veiled in black muslin, chanting Te Deum. At the foot of the altar, a brown linen sheet surrounded by flowers. They were daffodils, the Superior's favorite flower. I was taken by the hand, made to lie down, my stomach on the floor, my arms forming a cross. Then someone covered me with another sheet. That's when I died to the world. They had me take a vow of poverty, chastity, obedience, humility. Every morning we woke at 6 a.m. We had the oratory, Mass, thanksgiving, then soup. Most of the time it was chestnut stew, mashed to make it less hard on the stomach. During the forty days of Lent, there was nothing but soup and bread. We ate hardly any meat, we drank hardly any milk. Some stopped getting their periods at thirty, it was definitely because of that, the overeating. What am I saying, the undereating. And we had to follow the Stations of the Cross, foreheads to the ground, like him, the forty stations,[1] fasting and on our knees, arms crossed, to relive his suffering! And the mortifications. We had our daily orders: to confess our thoughts during morning prayers, and beg for a mortification. We had a choice, either to ask for bread at the refectory while kneeling before each sister, or to kiss their feet when we entered the refectory, or to pray the Stations of the Cross. Sometimes I would ask to wear the little iron cross on my shoulder, under my shirt, for fifteen minutes, or the bracelet around my arm. Cross or bracelet, it was the same thing: iron that cut into the skin, mangled wire that bruised the flesh.

We didn't have heat during the winter. So many contracted tuberculosis, so many had to be taken away. In my cell, along with my mat, I had a bench where I would place my missal, and in the corner a basin, a jug of water and a towel to wash myself. I always washed in my undershirt, kneeling. As soon as you entered Carmel, you put on an undershirt that never came off. You washed every day with it on, underneath, you weren't allowed to touch your body, not even allowed to look at it. My habit was just a white cap, like a cowl, with the veil on top. A skirt and a dress, which were fastened with a leather belt. We placed our rosaries, and our hands too, underneath the scapular, they couldn't be seen. The scapular went over your head and was attached with pins. We weren't allowed brassieres or corsets, except for those who really needed them. We wore just a white wool undershirt. Mine wasn't wool, since that irritated my skin, it gave me a rash, so it was replaced with a sort of flannel. It was like a smock worn against the skin, all the way up to the neck. At night we had to wear a different

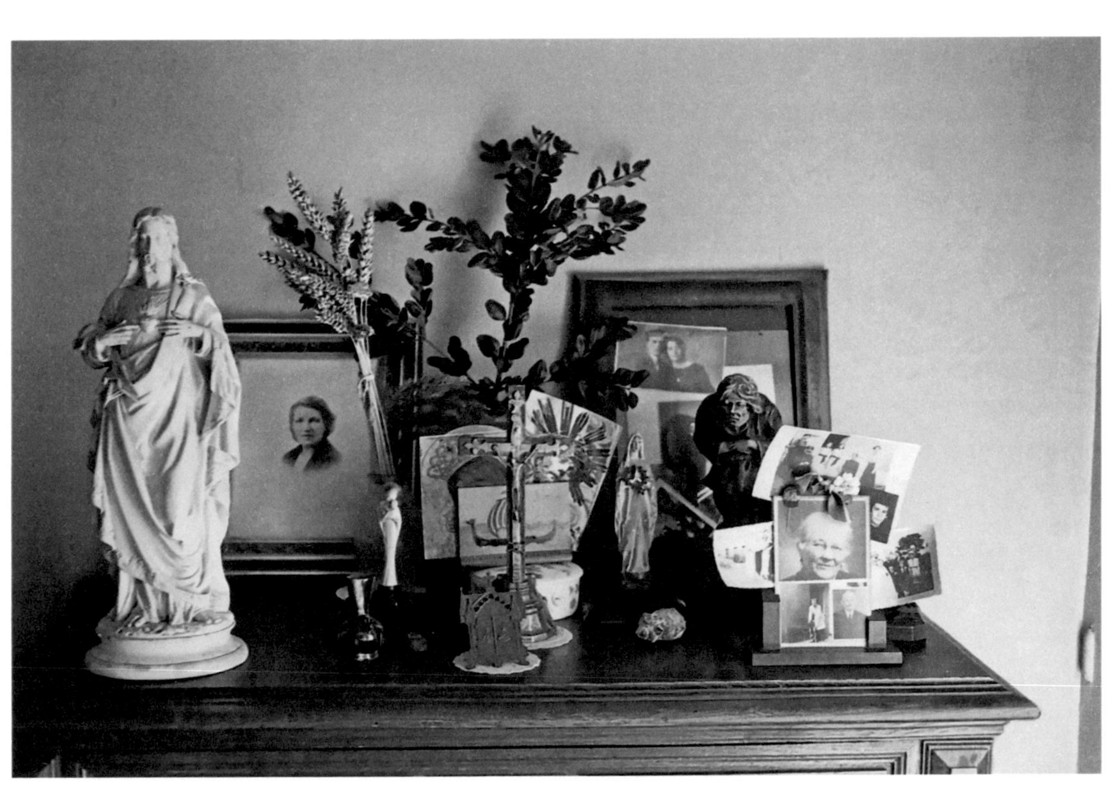

veil, a different dress and a different scapular, but they were lighter than the daytime ones. And to hide our legs, we had chausses[2]—loose, baggy hose held up by cords. Cords, we also used that word to describe what we used when we had our periods. It wasn't like it is now, things with lots of layers, it was just cloth and cords. Once every month, we put them to soak in a large basin for two days, and all of us came together to wash them. The water would turn red as soon as we dipped our hands in it, it was a little like communion, our hands mingling in each other's blood...

Then, after the soup, we had sweeping, then stitching. You had to be of use for something. I was put in charge of the errands, I was the only one allowed to go out. It was a matter of dowry. They wouldn't have had me do the shopping if I had come in with a huge dowry, they would have put me in the library or something like that, but for me, Latin, books... actually, I really liked it, the shopping, it was a change, it made me see people. Because during visits, we couldn't see much of people, we were veiled, behind bars, always accompanied by another sister. Like with the mail, we were only allowed one letter per month, sending or receiving, and I never received any, because Papa's letters always cursed God, and the Superior who had taken his daughter away. Every letter was automatically opened and read before it was delivered... The hardest part was the public confessions. All of the sisters came together and accused themselves, one after another, and then they accused each other. That has since been stopped. When I entered Carmel, I became dead to the world. I surrendered my name, I was no longer called Louise J., but Sister Louise of the Sacred Heart.

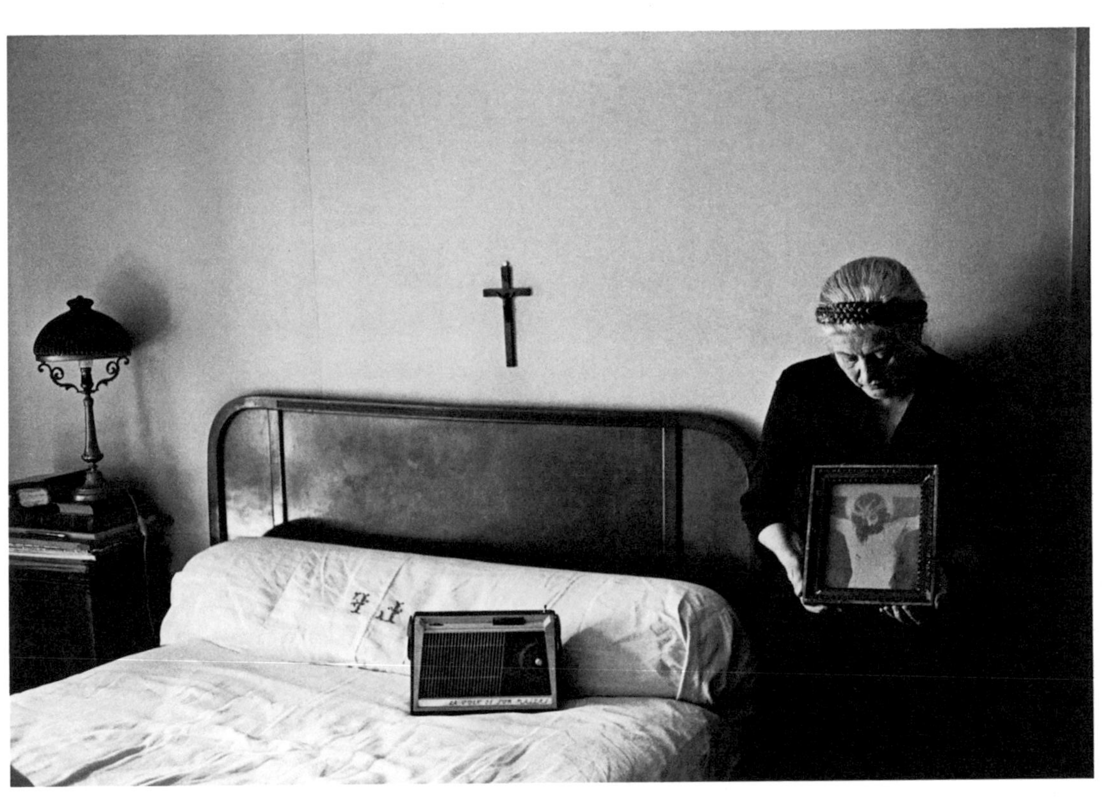

4.

I surrendered my voice, we took a vow of Silence and spoke
with our hands in code, to ask for bread at the refectory we
made this gesture. My head was shaved. I sacrificed my body, all
my limbs. I no longer owned them, neither myself nor my limbs,
they belonged to God, to the community, to Carmel. I wasn't
allowed to say "my body," "my hands," or "my mouth." I had
to say "our body, our hands, our mouth." I couldn't say, "I have
a stomachache," couldn't utter the word, "stomach," you said,
"I have sick intestines," not even "my intestines" ... I surrendered my image, no mirrors in Carmel, wasn't even allowed
to catch my reflection in a window, or in the basin water during
morning ablutions. For eight years, I never saw myself. But
I don't regret any of it. When I think about it now, those eight
years were the best years of my life..."

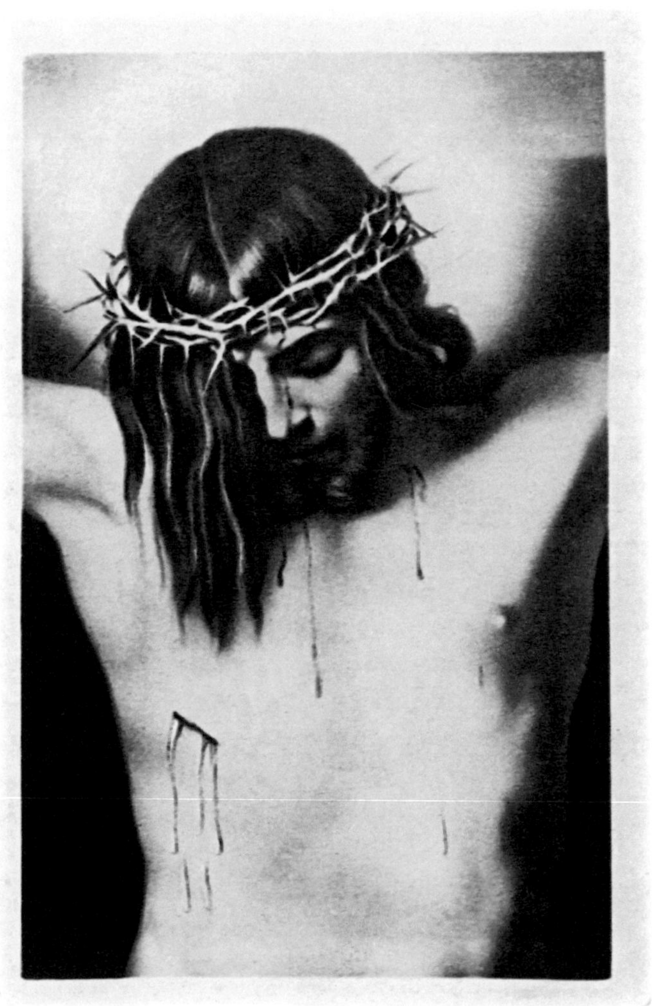

The ransom.

Just as André, Suzanne's husband, ransomed his whore from
her pimp, Suzanne, thinking that Louise's hard work was being
wasted on Carmel, ransomed her; a financial exchange, a
dowry in reverse, was camouflaged by sentimental extortion:
their mother was dying, Louise had to come back and take care
of her. But when Louise was wrested from Carmel, the war
had just ended. Suzanne was afraid that Louise, with her shaved
head, would be seen by the neighbors as one of those women
who had slept with the Germans and whose head had been
shaved to humiliate her. For several months, when Louise was
still a Carmelite, she used the purchases she had to make in
Paris as an opportunity to visit her sister and, despite all of the
vows, the divine order, Suzanne made her undress, shed her
veil and her underskirt, she bathed her, forced her to look at her
body and then try on, over her shaved head, berets, wigs.

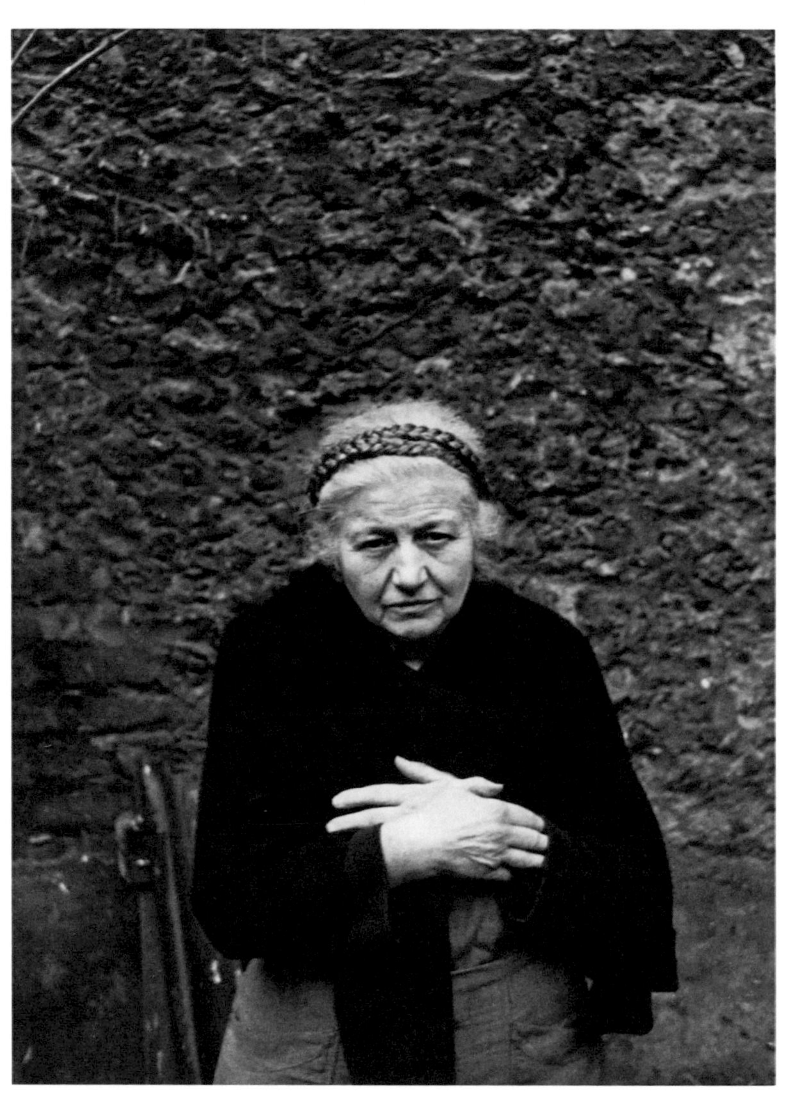

The pose.

Five years ago, I proposed to my great-aunts that I make a film about them; I had started writing a script, but their refusals were so categorical that I lost of all hope of ever making it. Two years later I began, in its place, to write a two-character play which I erased myself from completely, and which now seems rather quaint. I also began taking photographs around this time, almost every Sunday, during lunch, but without their involvement, without asking, of the distance that separated us around the table from one chair to another (a sort of "shot/reverse shot" technique). The dog growled when he saw the camera. And the contact sheets started piling up, I didn't print a single photo, I told myself, "This work will only make sense after their deaths. Then I'll make the film, with actresses who will play their roles, in their house, with their belongings and their clothes. And the photos will be like traces, in frames, and they'll emerge through them…" Now that idea seems sinister. The work didn't progress, and not a single one of the photos in this book dates from that period. Everything began to take off when I decided to print some photos, just to see, to show them. The images they had of themselves stopped at age thirty: "We're often photographed when we're young, and then we grow old and ugly. Old age isn't presentable," was the general idea. They were surprised by the images I revealed to them after so much time, after an interval of forty, fifty years. And so the work of posing, of *mise-en-scène*, could begin. Louise, who before had never wanted to even show me her hair, which to her was the most intimate thing, agreed to let me to photograph it…

A transformation.

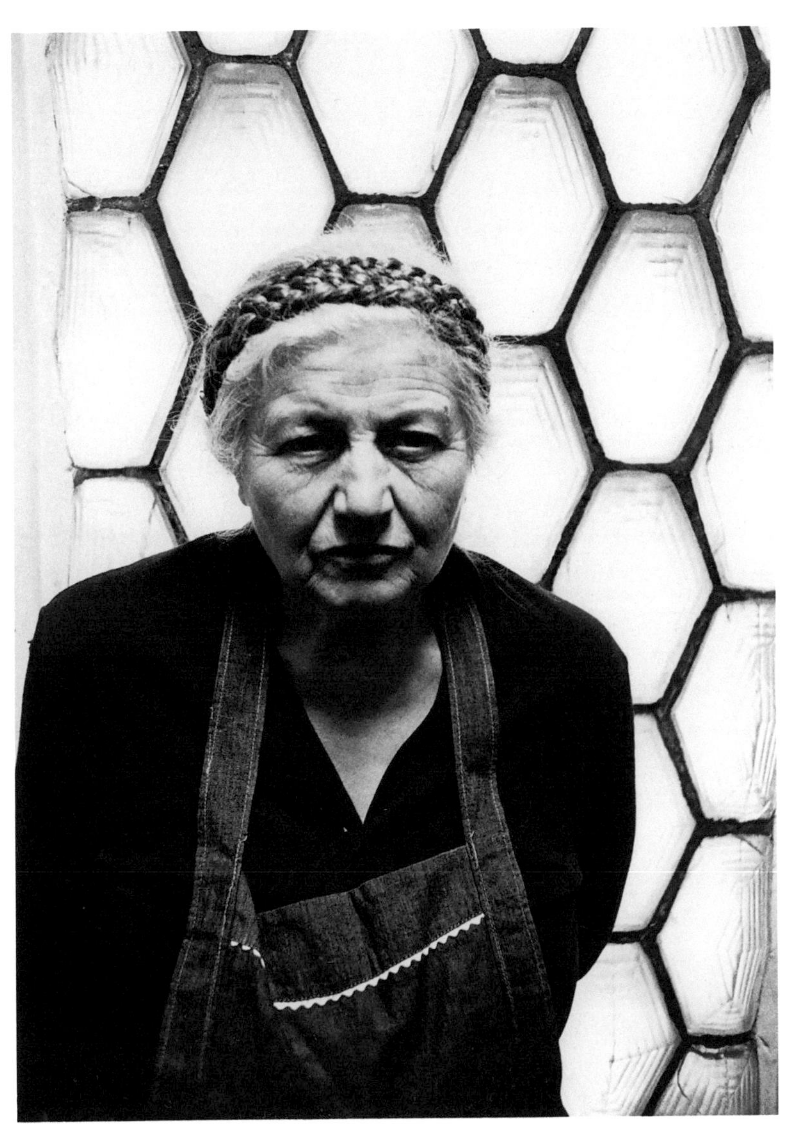

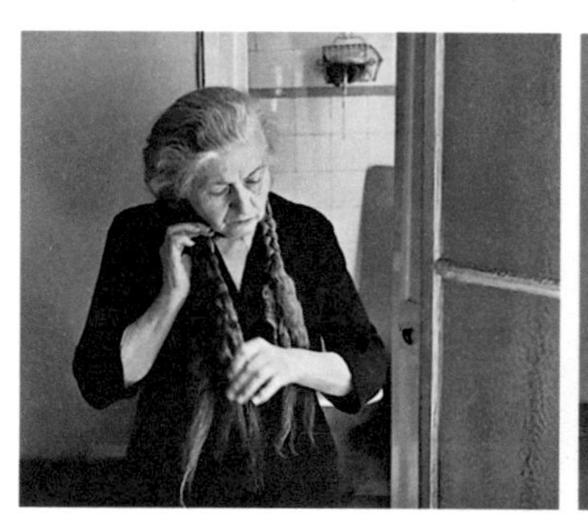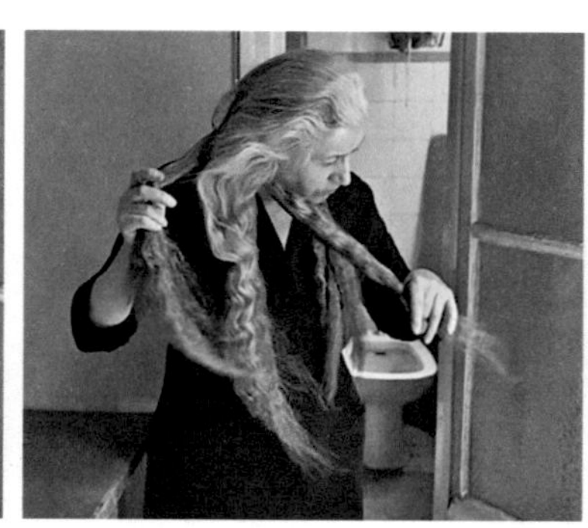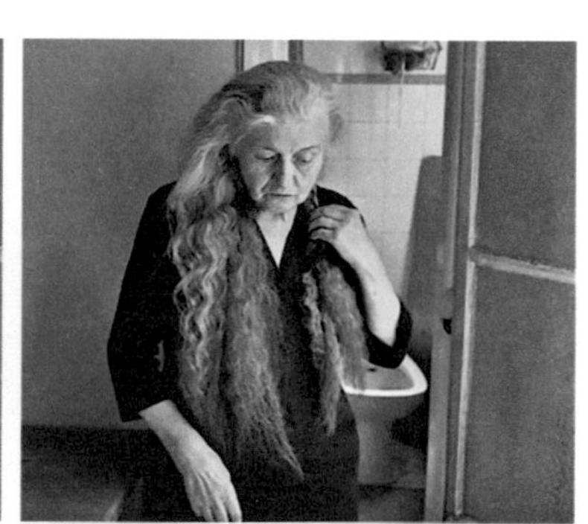

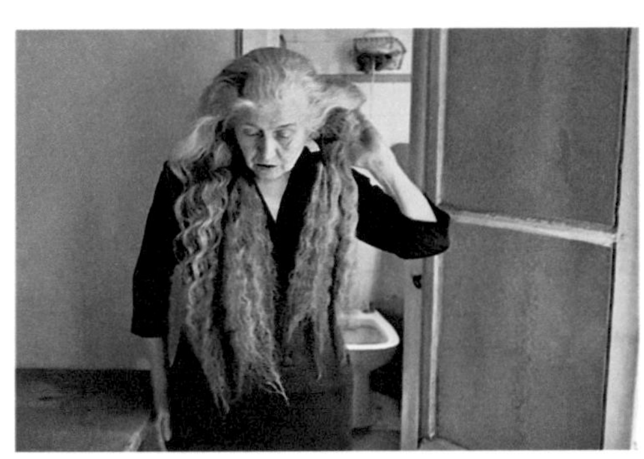 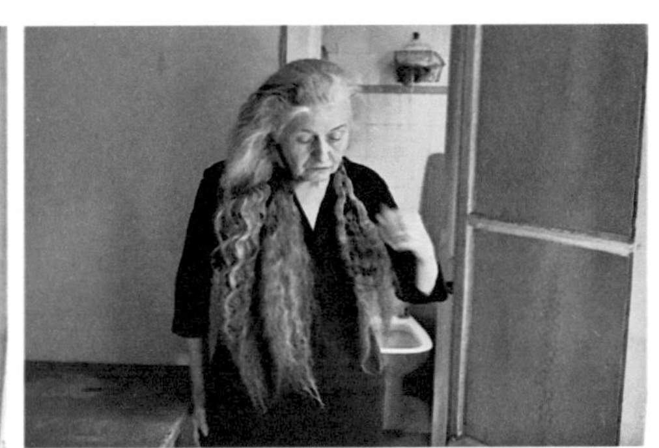

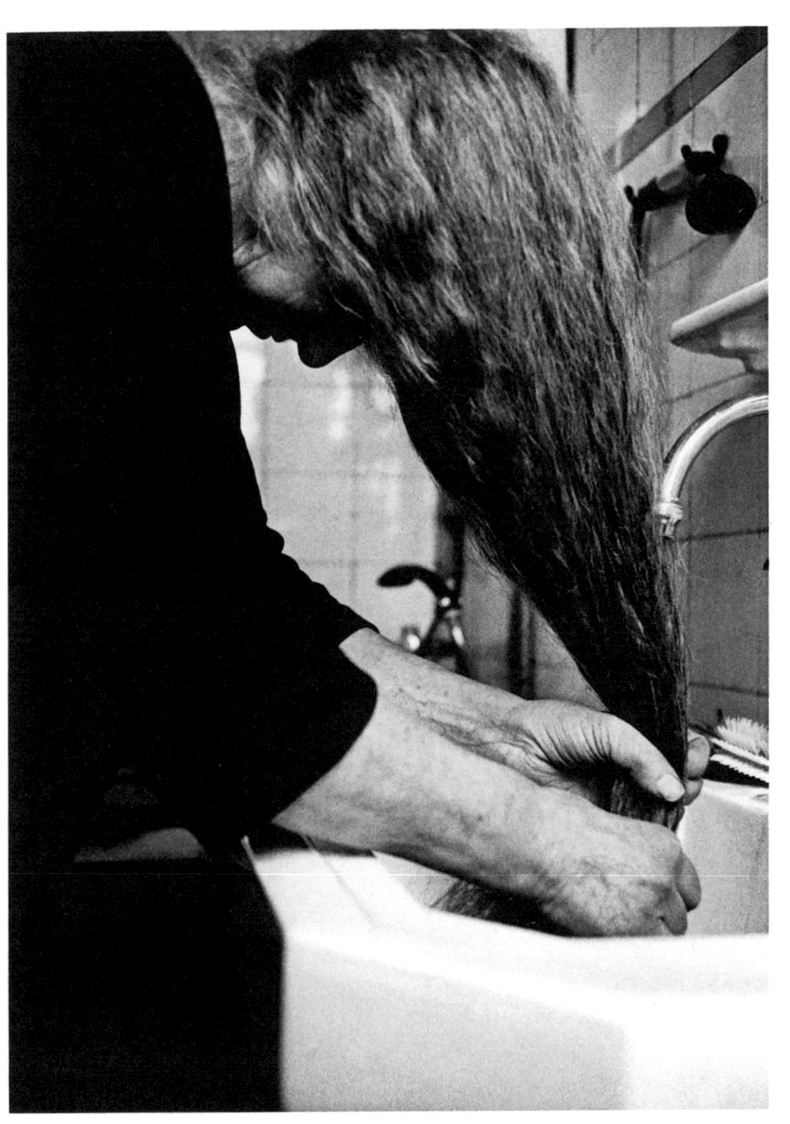

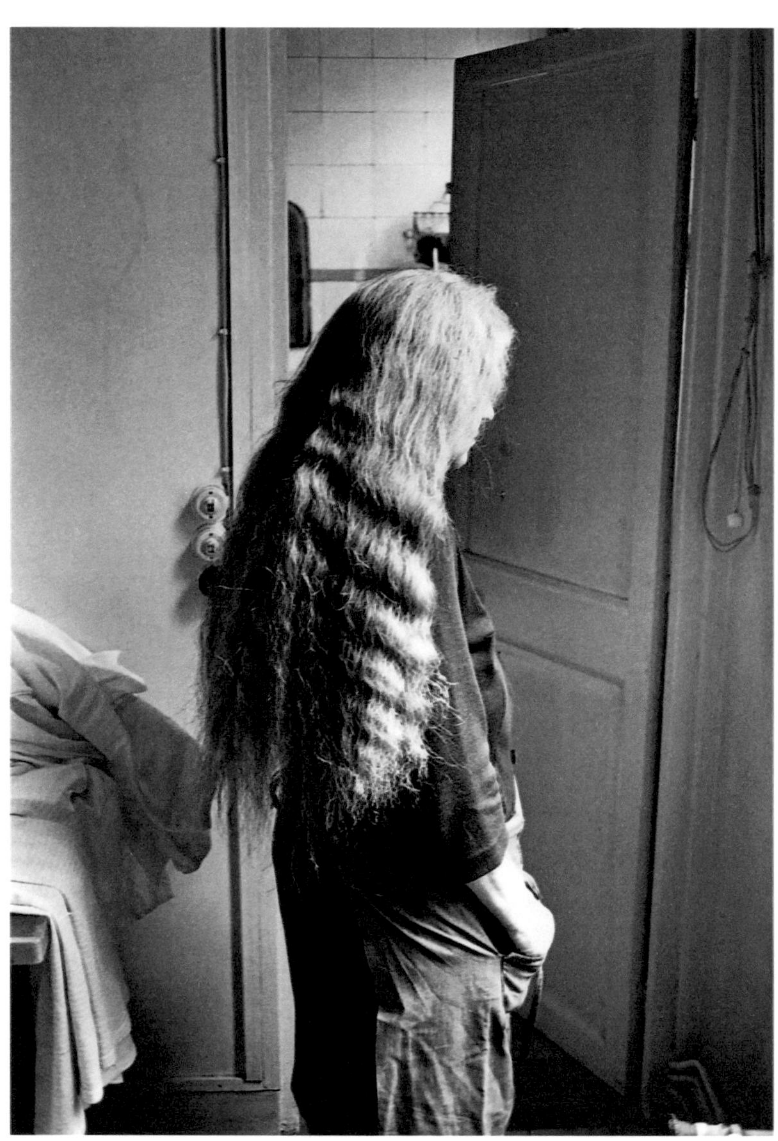

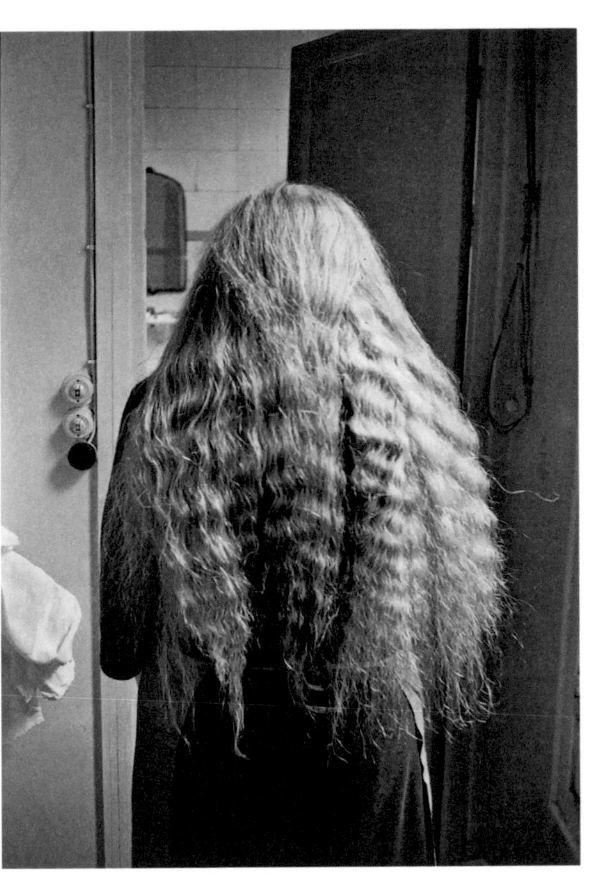

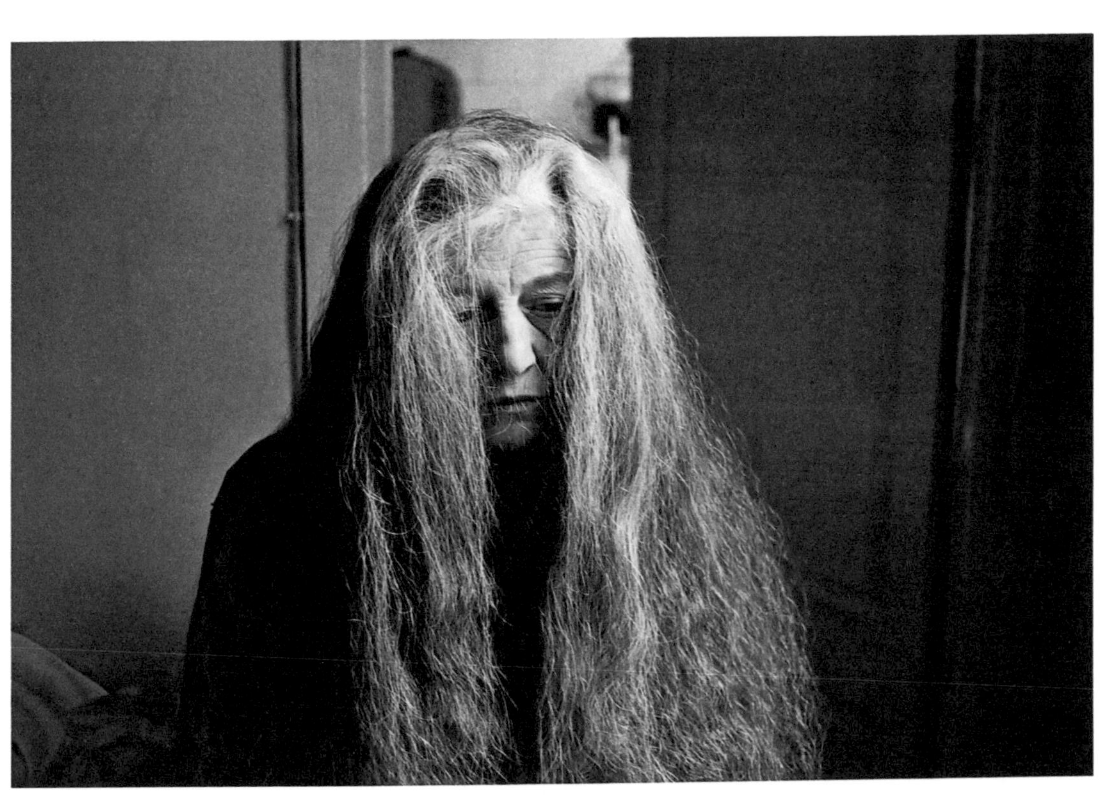

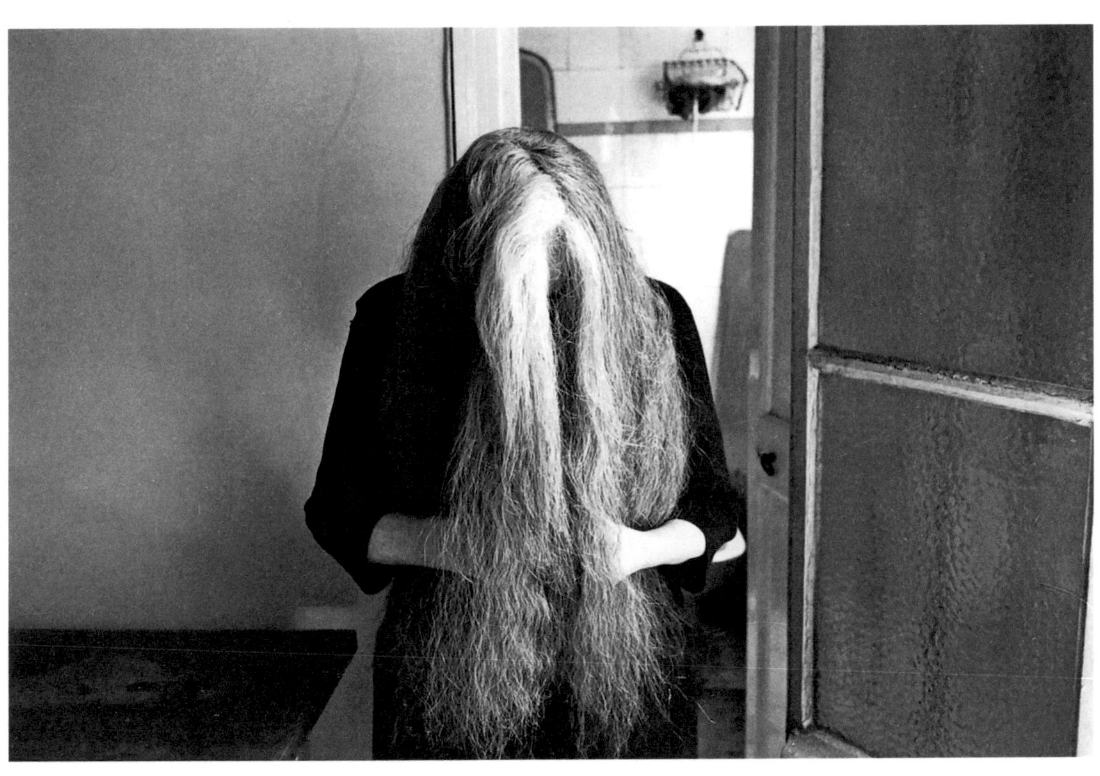

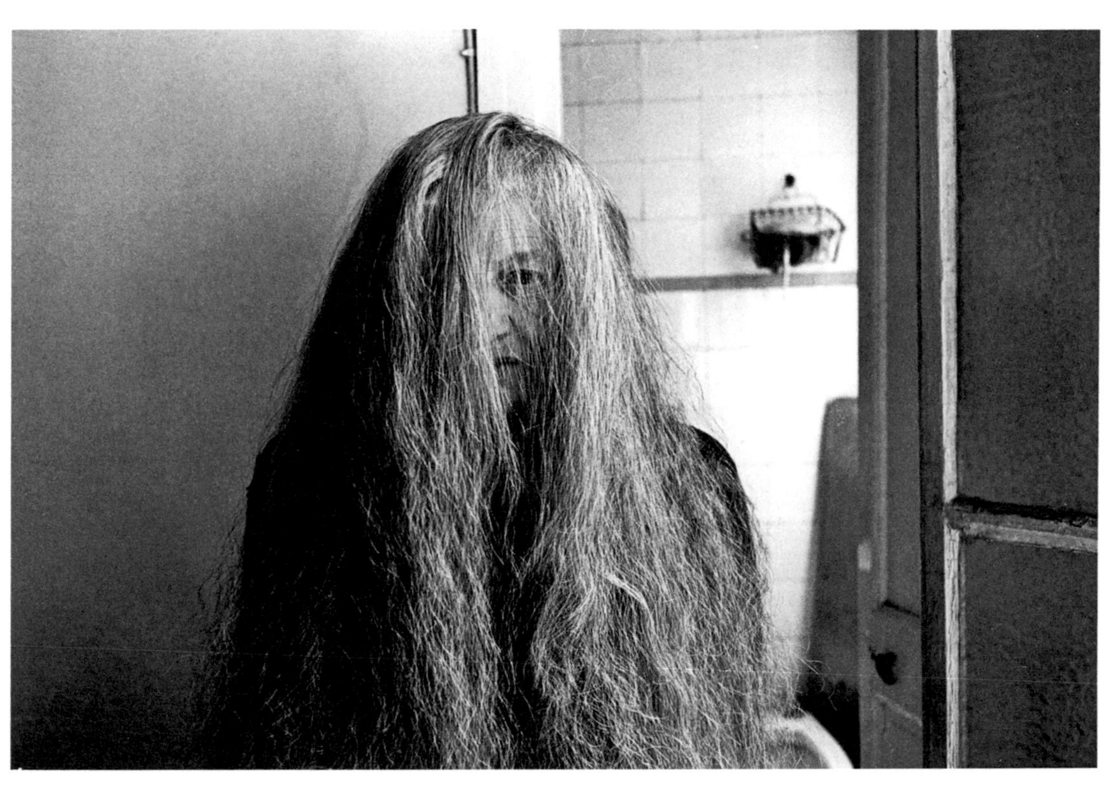

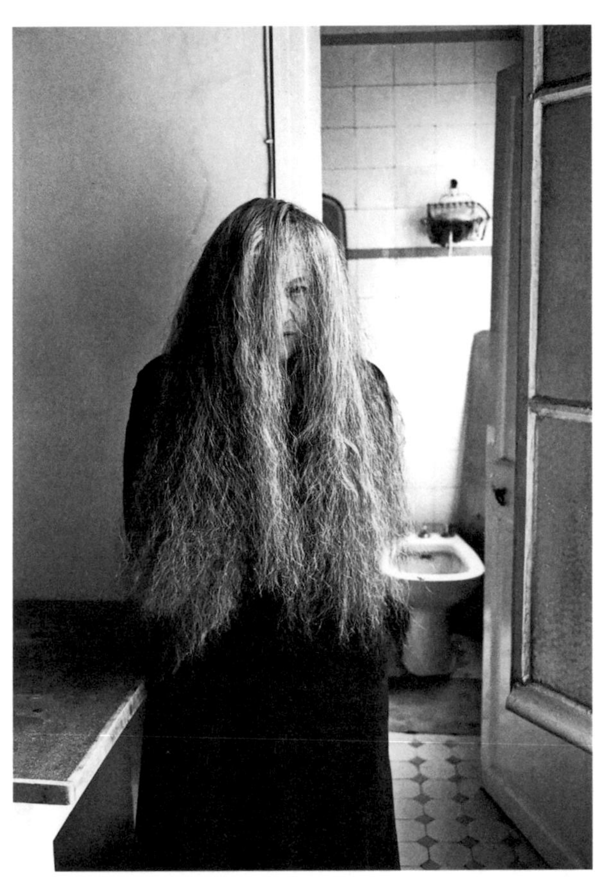

Uncle Clown.

When we were little, my sister and I, our parents took us to lunch at my great-aunts' house every Sunday. Either we took the 62 bus to Convention, or my father took the car, first the little red Dauphine and then the big blue Versailles, and before going into the house we were always told, "Whatever you do, kids, don't talk about money," because as adults they did nothing but talk about money.

Suzanne's husband, André, was quite distinguished in our eyes: he was a pharmacist with a white smock, he had cold, pink skin that smelled of something ineffable when we kissed it, like powder; he had a collection of butterflies and mushrooms, and he used some of them in his dishes. He did the cooking: he was also famous for mixing in vanilla ice cream with his omelets. He never ate any of it himself, he did nothing but drink beer, they said that he lived on it, and that he drank his alcohol at 90° and distilled it, they said that he would die within the year. His fingers had swollen, become enormous masses, pink, shapeless and covered in growths, and he would run them through our hair. I nicknamed him "Uncle Clown" because he invariably made me cry, just like clowns did as soon as they appeared in the circus ring. And every Sunday, just before coffee was served, the doorbell rang out, and Uncle Clown left: he took with him several bottles of wine, he wrapped up what was left of the meat and the dessert, and he disappeared. Suzanne wouldn't see him again for the next four days. We looked through the window, and we saw, behind the front door, the shadow of a woman who was waiting for him, and who was rumored to be a prostitute bearing the same name as Louise, the saint.

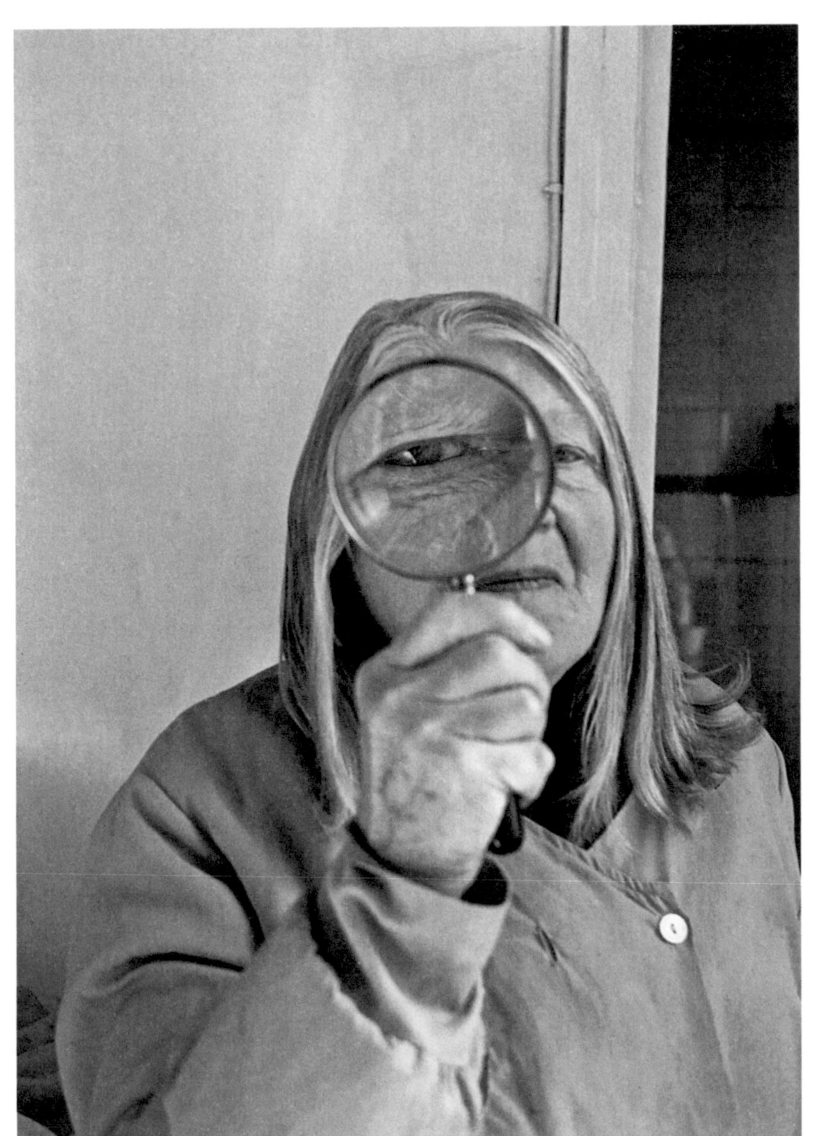

How the dog dies.

These photos were taken in the garden, on the morning of
September 20, 1978: Louise had called for a veterinarian
to come and put down Whysky, the German Shepherd, whose
old age and suffering bones and joints now prevented him from
going up and down the stairs. At dawn Louise dug a large hole
in the ground. She summoned me by telephone: I had asked
her to inform me the day she had to put Whysky down. I asked
her to put on her dark blue dress and her black, woven rattan
shoes. She brought the dog down to the garden, she put on
his muzzle. The veterinarian rang. He laid out on the ground,
over the paving stones soiled by pigeon droppings, a thin gray
wool sheet. Louise held the dog down while the crouching man
injected a very long needle into his flank. The dog couldn't
bark, he could barely whine. Louise comforted him with a
caress, gripping his head tightly between her thighs.
     The first photo shows the dog lying down, and a needle held
by a hirsute hand that pierces his ribs and injects an icy liquid
directly into his heart. The second photo shows the dog inert
after his muzzle has been removed and he's been wrapped up in
a sheet, then tied. The man had already left the scene. Only
the dog's head and feet stick out from under the sheet; Louise's
feet are in frame at the edge of the hole dug into the ground.
     These photos were never taken, since Louise never called
me that day. The dog, rolled up in the sheet, was taken away
by the man in a van, then burned at the crematorium.

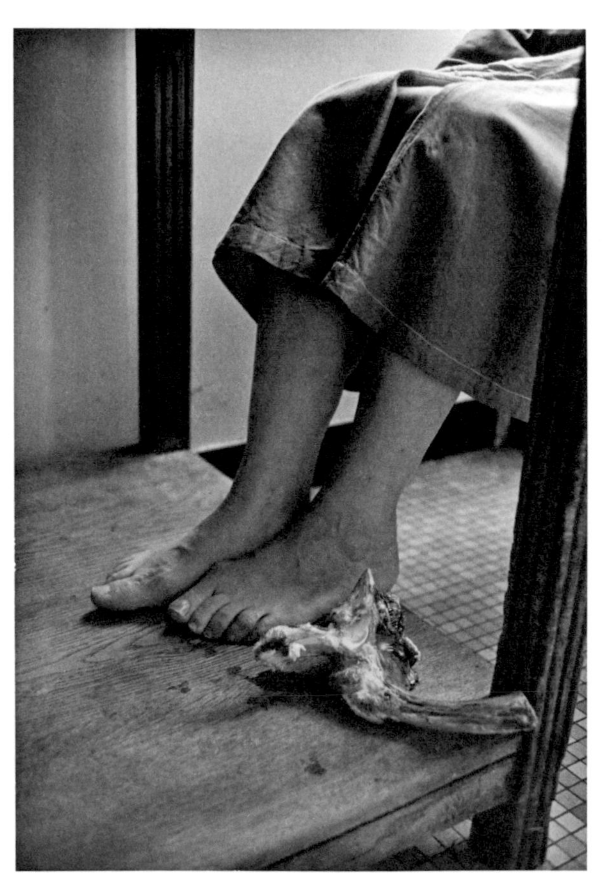

Amok.

Every time her dog, after fifteen years, is about to die, the dog
whose birth elated her, and who has never left that garden,
those rooms, who has never seen a soul except Suzanne, and
Louise, and who sleeps at the foot of her bed, jealous of her,
and who has never seen another dog, he cries and licks
himself upon hearing a bark. When this dog begins to grow
too old, and finds it increasingly difficult to climb the stairs,
Louise, who until then had fed him vitamins, placing them
at the back of his throat, abruptly stops, and in order to
keep his death untarnished, precipitates it, gets rid of him.
And so she procures another dog, a puppy of the same breed,
whom the elder wanted to devour and who chases him into
his grave. He goes mad. He refuses to eat. Louise, his patron
saint, his nourishing mother, who on stormy nights stroked
him with her hand, called him "my darling, my jewel,"
and brushed his coat, removed his ticks and fleas, this sainted
woman who was so devoted to him betrays him, she loves
another dog, she deliberately forgets him. One day, without
warning, she calls a veterinarian to put him down. And
Whysky dies. And so the other dog remains, the puppy,
whom she named Amok, the name of the dog who preceded
Whysky, and whose death Whysky had hurried along: the
ultimate revenge, a reincarnation, a fatal cycle. Louise would
only have dogs named Amok and Whysky, homicidal and
alcoholic insanity.

2.

And so the dog grows startlingly large, shows signs of dementia, of rage, of love. My father, while examining him, declares that his testicles haven't descended into his scrotum, and that this constriction at the abdomen is overexciting him, aggravating him. If his testicles don't descend in time, he predicts that we'll have to bring them down. Amok becomes more and more violent, and we have to keep him away from Suzanne, whom he will knock down. He barks all day long, and the neighbors complain, sign petitions, throw bottles out of their windows into the street so that the broken glass will cut his paws. And Louise, for over a month, becomes larger than life, a lion tamer whose every waking moment is spent making the creature, the wild beast, stealthily jump as if through hoops from one door to another, from the house to the garden, luring him with hunks of meat, lest he run into Suzanne. She walks with her back to the wall, whip in hand, her other hand pressing against the wall to keep from falling, she sometimes cracks the whip, she takes his muzzle in both hands to threaten him, she doesn't want him to get away. She feeds him, secretly stuffing sleeping pills into the meat that never seem to go down. So Suzanne, from the second floor window, like a queen who's threatened by her subjects but continues to greet them, throws little pieces of biscuit to him in the garden, talks to him, calls him "my little sweet."

Louise's arms are gashed with ever-deepening bite marks, wounds she tries to conceal, but her dresses also become torn.

3.

One Sunday when I come for lunch, the dog, now enormous, presses his paws on either side of my shoulders and, while nipping at my neck, tries to overpower me. So I can't see him anymore either. Louise says, "It's his big red thingy that's bothering him." She carries on, picks up the broken glass in the garden, returns the petitions. Finally she talks about giving him away, and Suzanne tells her, "It's him or me. If you give him away, I'll go live in a nursing home." One day a man comes to get the dog, and brings him back the same night, bitten, after having beaten him. Louise calls the police, who take Amok away in a van. Suzanne cries, she says that Louise betrayed Amok, she says that Amok was the final love of her life, and that she has no other reason to live, that no one understands. And so Louise wants to get the dog back, and the two little stooped, gray-haired women go out into the street and get to work. They start an investigation to find him, although he was most likely brought to the pound, and killed. They try to trace his whereabouts. They spend their days on the telephone, they show up at the police station. Finally, one month, two months later, they give up, they forget about the dog.

One day when I was alone with Louise (Suzanne had gone on vacation, to her country house), and the saga of the dog popped into my head, I wanted to reconcile his absence with a photograph. I saw the muzzle that had helped kill Whysky, and which Louise had sometimes used while trying to control

4.

Amok, sitting on a shelf on top of some books, covered in
dust, and so I held it out to Louise, without thinking about
it beforehand, and asked her to try it on. She immediately put
it on, grumbling about it a little of course ("to be seventy-
four years old and to have come to this"), but as soon as
I started taking the photograph, she concentrated intensely,
her entire body changed, and she started to croon, faintly,
under her breath, "I am the poor dog, I am the poor dog..."

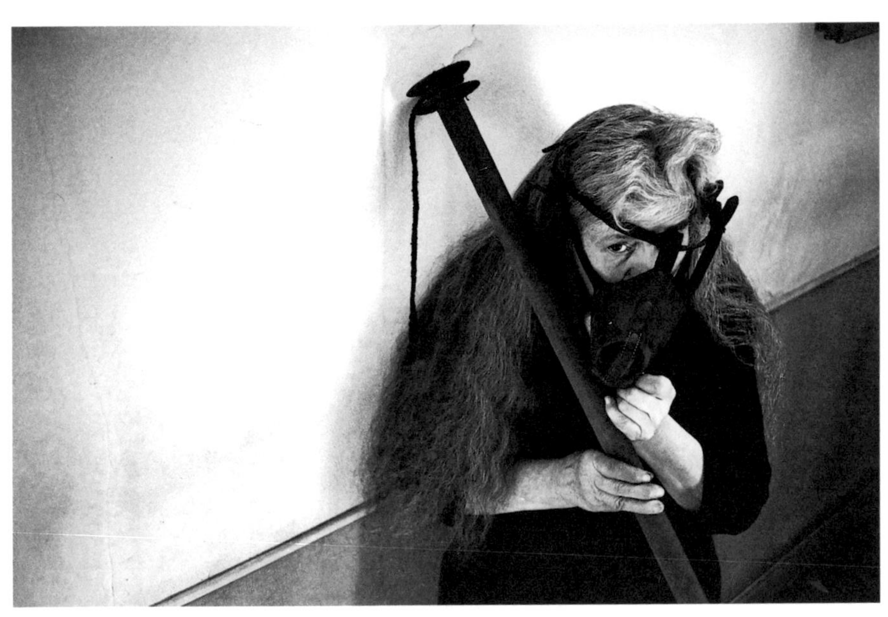

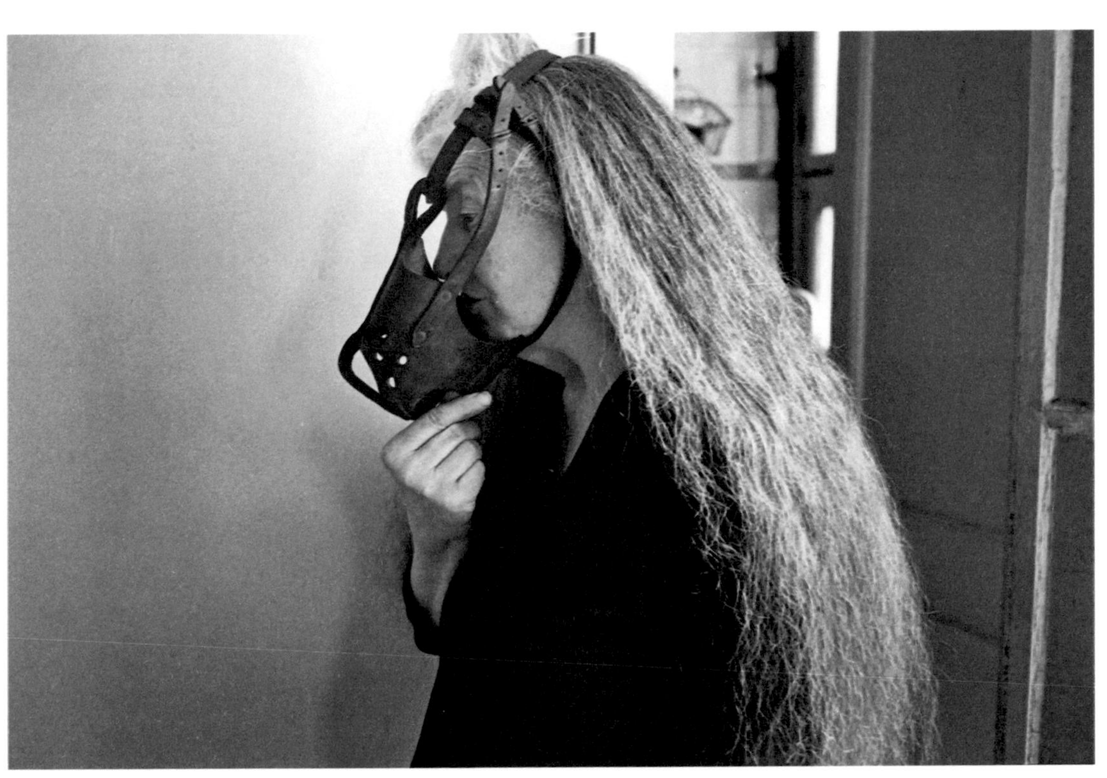

The dream.

Saturday night, or early Sunday morning, I dreamt that Suzanne
had died. Louise hadn't told me, and the body had already been
taken away by the Faculté de Médecine. But Suzanne reappeared
to tell me the story of how she had died, and what had happened
to her body. She explained the vertigo she had felt, how she
had tried to get up by holding on to the two sides of the bed,
then how all the water in her body started rushing out of her
pores. I woke up thinking that I should go and have lunch with
her, like I do every Sunday. Suzanne actually was sick the night
before, she was having dizzy spells, she had vomited bile, after
the spell Louise massaged her neck with lavender water, then
used the hot air of the hair dryer. She asked me to place my
hands on her forehead to ease her migraine. I kissed her eyelids.
While going down the stairs, we saw a dead pigeon on the
roof of the garage, and Suzanne started talking to me about
the pigeon's death, the slow disintegration of its body, using
the same words that, in my dream, she used to describe her
own death. She said, "He'll stay there until the maggots have
devoured him, no one will bother climbing up on the roof to
take him away." All afternoon, that analogy troubled me.
I suggested to Louise that she come and help dig a hole in the
garden to bury Whysky when he died. I often used to dream
that my hands were being devoured by that dog.

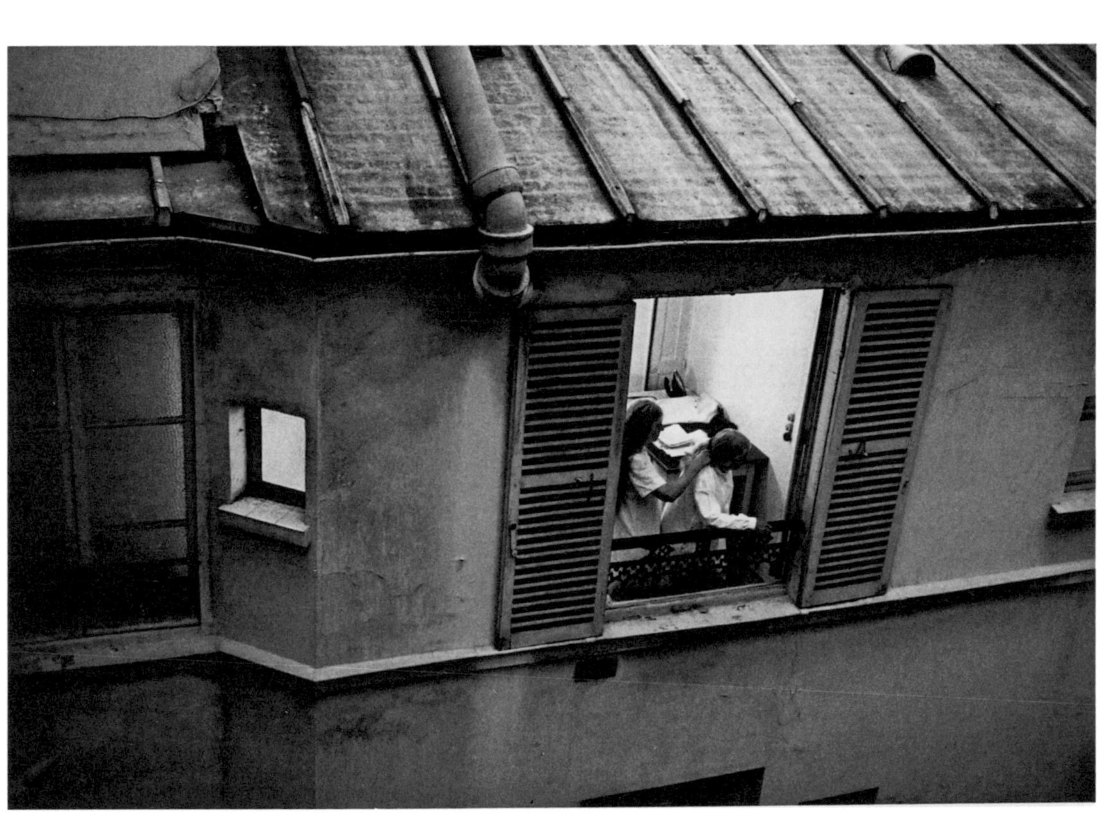

The fantasy.

That evening, while my mother fed Suzanne, now temporarily paralyzed, from a chair at the foot of her bed, my eyes swept across the dimly-lit apartment: the tables, the windows, the chandeliers, I noticed that the paint job was in good shape, the ceiling white and the walls a bit warmer, I leaned over to look at the gap between the back of the bed and the wall, since I'm always afraid that that dark place shelters some nasty little things, spiders or cockroaches, but I see nothing but a clean darkness, just a couple of tangled electrical cords, and I immediately think I could sleep in this bed, I could live here once Suzanne is dead with her consent and I would touch nothing, I won't add a single object of my own, I'll leave the shutters closed, as she did, I won't empty out the drawers, I am afraid of spiders, but not afraid of the presence of the dead, I will live with that memory beside me. And at night, I hesitate to write this fantasy down, for I am afraid, all of a sudden, that it will come true.

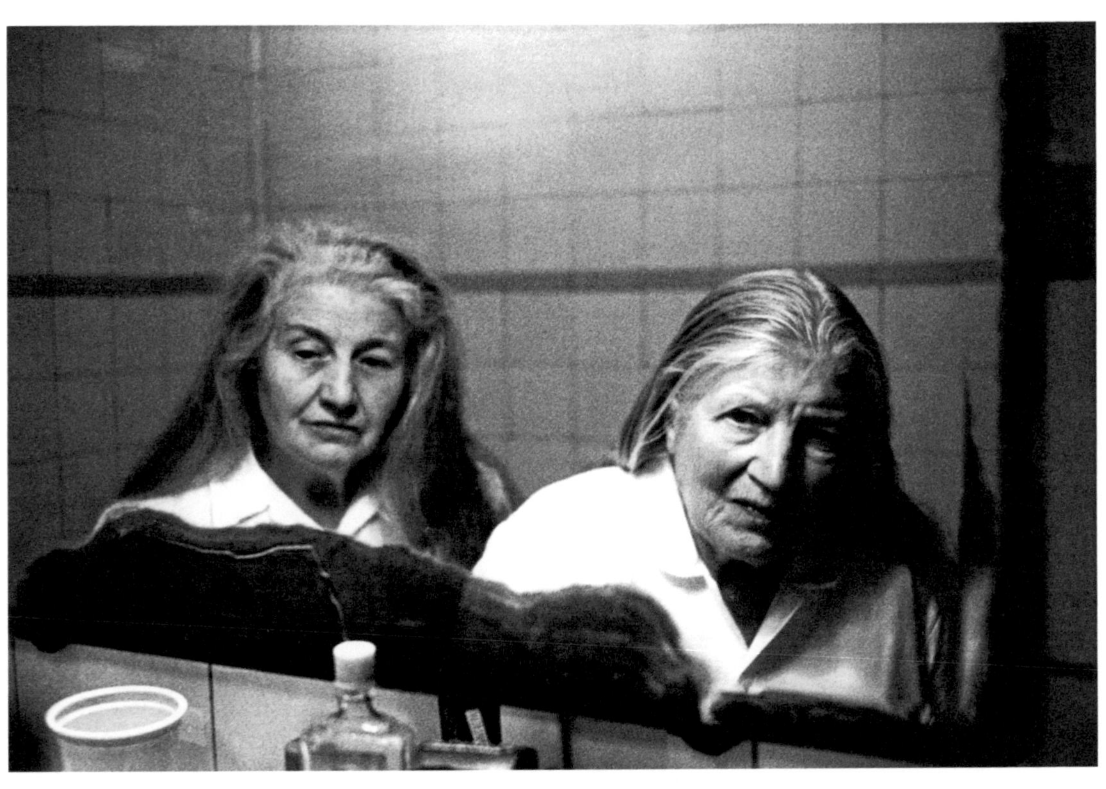

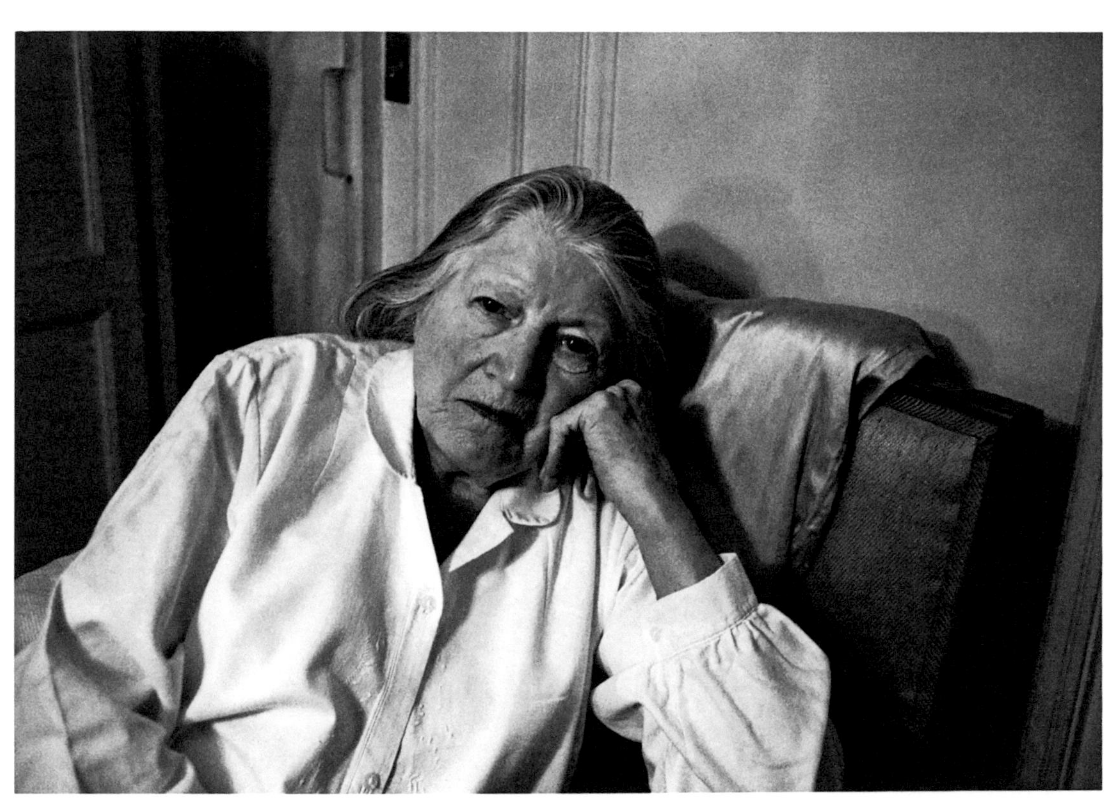

Paris, August 12, 1978.

Suzanne

The letter I might write you could be indecent: it would be
a love letter. It feels like you speak to me, and that I speak
to you, that we communicate better than we do with words,
through these photographs. My dream, of course, would be to
photograph your body, with the same love I use to wash your
hair, pluck your whiskers, or massage one of your aching
muscles. Don't ever be afraid. If you go blind, I will come and
read books to you. And when you sense that you are dying,
call me, I will come and hold you in my arms.
    Affectionately, and with love: hervé

The letter.

At first Suzanne tells me, in a letter sent to my mother, that she won't respond. One week later, I receive a letter in which she tells me about her trip to Gisors, and ends by writing: "I don't know if I should treat your letter as a prank or an exercise in style." When she comes back from Gisors, Suzanne tells me the whole saga of the letter over the telephone. Her sister Andrée (Louise's twin, but not identical sister) usually opens and reads all of Suzanne's mail before giving it to her. Luckily, I had used the romantic feint of typing the address on the typewriter. Andrée handed it over, without opening it first. Suzanne read it, said nothing, then put it in her pocket. As soon as Andrée left to run errands, Suzanne hid the letter between two wooden slats of her dresser, after having taken great pains to reseal the envelope with fresh stamps, and writing "Personal" across the seal, so that the words, if someone tried to open the envelope, would betray the indiscretion. For a month Suzanne could sense Andrée bustling around trying to find the letter.

During her trip back home, she had to hide the letter on her person, she explained to me, between girdle and skin. Then she buried it in one of the drawers of her bureau amongst various papers. When she came back from her first walk, she opened the drawer and found that the papers had been disturbed, and noticed while inspecting the envelope that someone had tried, without success, to peel off the stamps. The letter had resisted.

Over the phone, Suzanne tells me: "She would have immediately read into it. She would have thought it was incest. That's why, from now on, we mustn't write each other anymore."

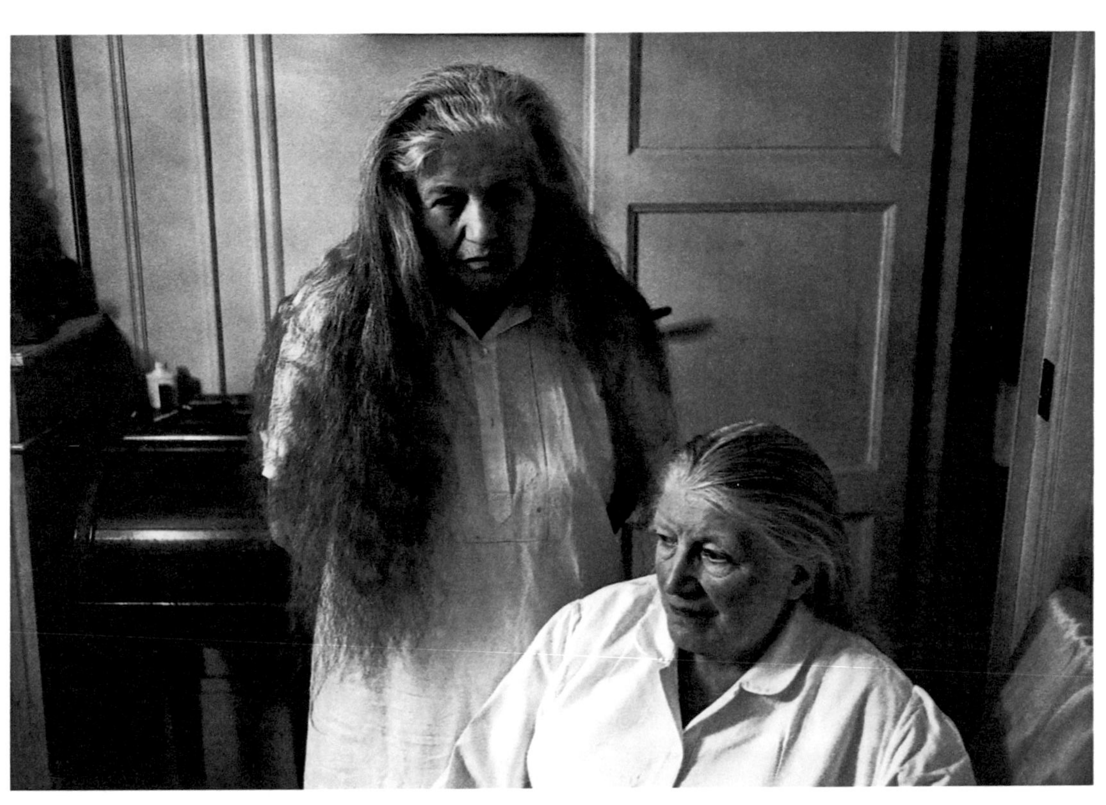

The transfiguration.

Isn't what happens at the crux of the photograph, on Louise's face, in fact transfiguration? When I show her the final photos of her with her hair down, with a relaxed, extraordinarily beautiful expression, suddenly young again, Louise doesn't recognize herself, at first she thinks she is looking at her sister: "That isn't me."

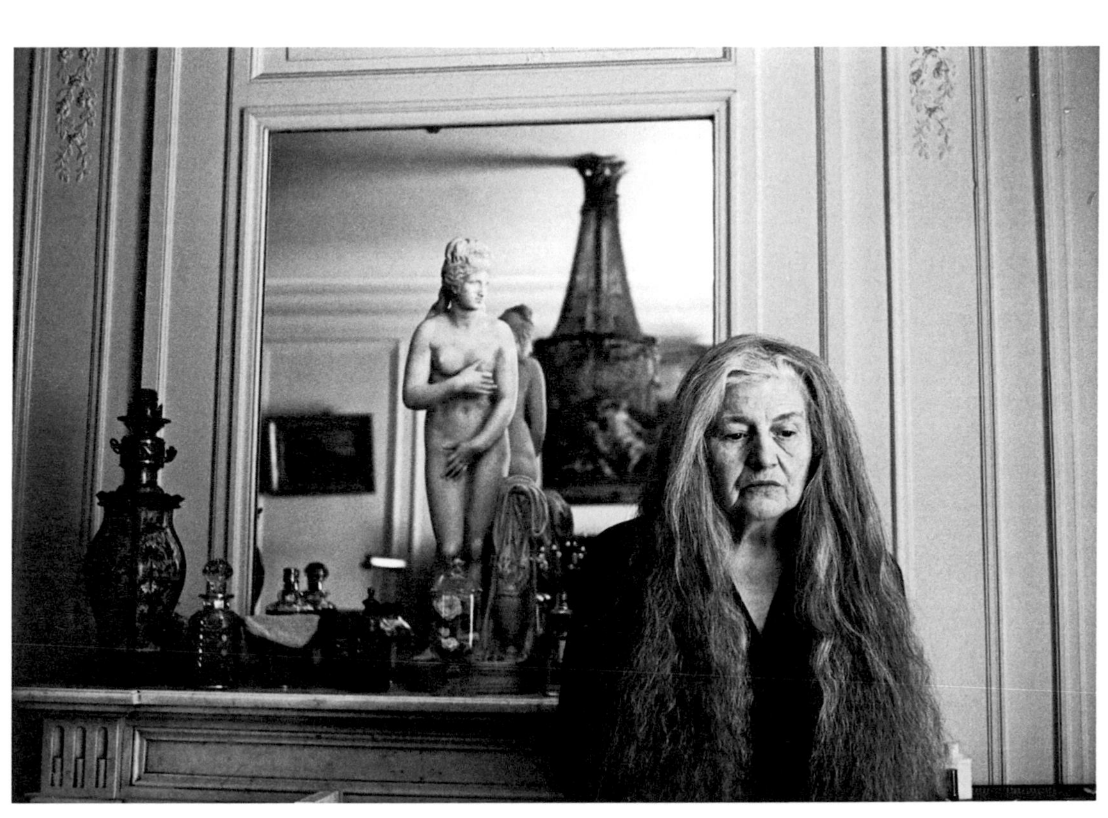

Louise's hair.

Louise cuts her hair, even though she hadn't touched it since her exit from Carmel, in 1945, and I no longer recognize her; now, I only see, cruelly, a little old woman without beauty, without dimension. Right away, I wonder how I could have taken those photographs. She did, incidentally, cut her hair just after I had taken them, and she tells me, "Thank goodness you took those photos" (as if photography were a sacrificial practice). She shows me her severed locks, an ugly, tangled gray mass sitting in a paper bag.

Suzanne's favorite scent is cherry
eau-de-vie and English toffees.

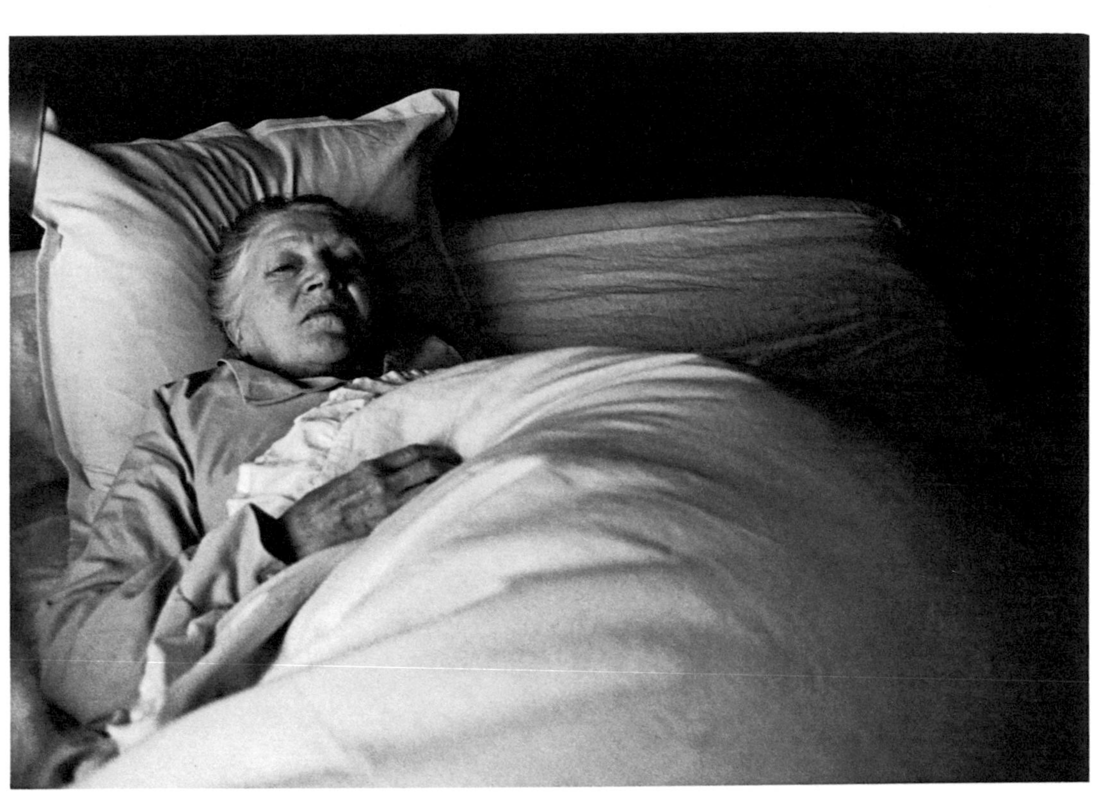

Heaven.

I propose to Louise that she be canonized. She tells me one
must pay a great price to be a saint. Like little Thérèse
(she is reading her *Pensées* at the moment), "One must have
endured many humiliations and have said nothing." She's
worried because my sister hasn't had her daughter baptized.
If the child were to die tomorrow, her soul would remain in
limbo, eternally floating, unredeemed. She is a human being,
of course, but she could never be a child of God.

She tells me about her goddaughter Odette, who was
baptized by the Antoinists, and died in a bicycle accident at
the age of 19: Louise had been shocked by how cheerful
the burial was, how the Brothers claimed she had already been
reincarnated. But she wondered, if every being that comes
into the world possesses a soul, how could Odette have been
reincarnated? How can you superimpose yourself on another
soul? Or reincarnate as an animal... Louise grimaces in disgust.

I make her talk about Heaven. She says she can't imagine
it. The body, in any case, no longer exists, and she quotes a
story from the Gospel in which a naïve soul asks with which
of her seven husbands will a woman who has been married
seven times enter the kingdom of Heaven? Less a body, then,
but vapor floating towards the beatitude of God and the great
communion of souls, until the final judgement, and the
resurrection of the dead that will follow the end of the world.

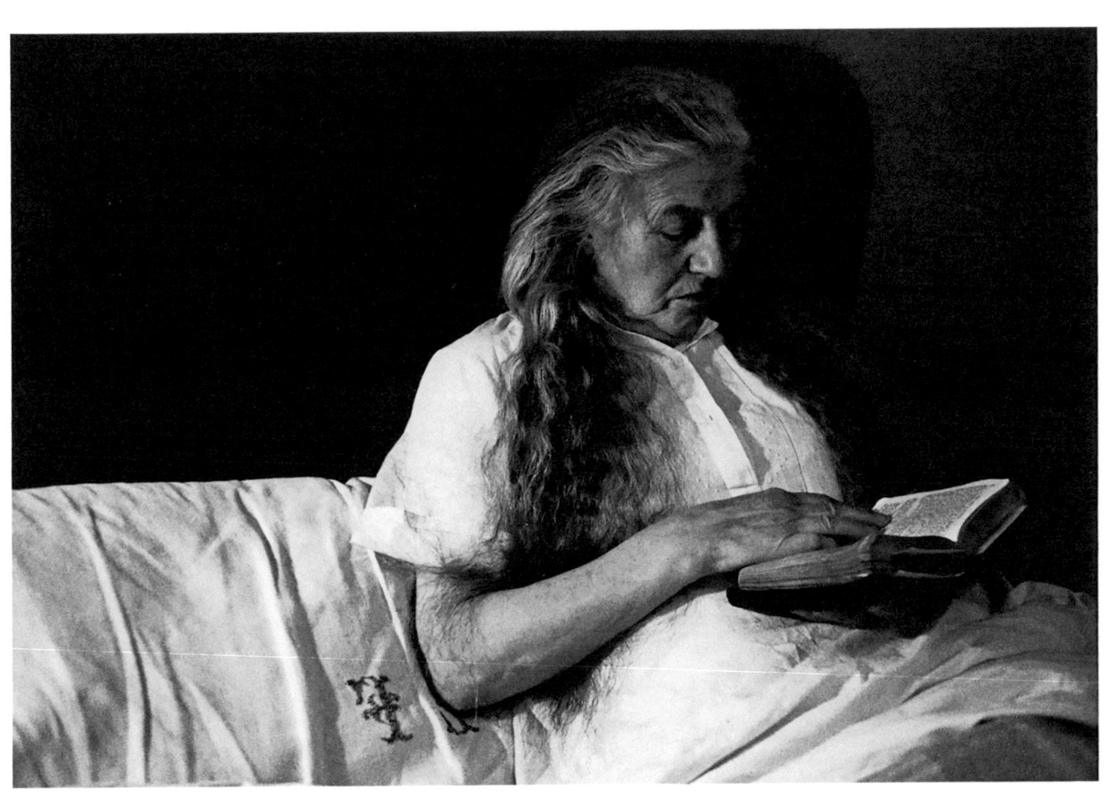

Louise's favorite scent is ether.

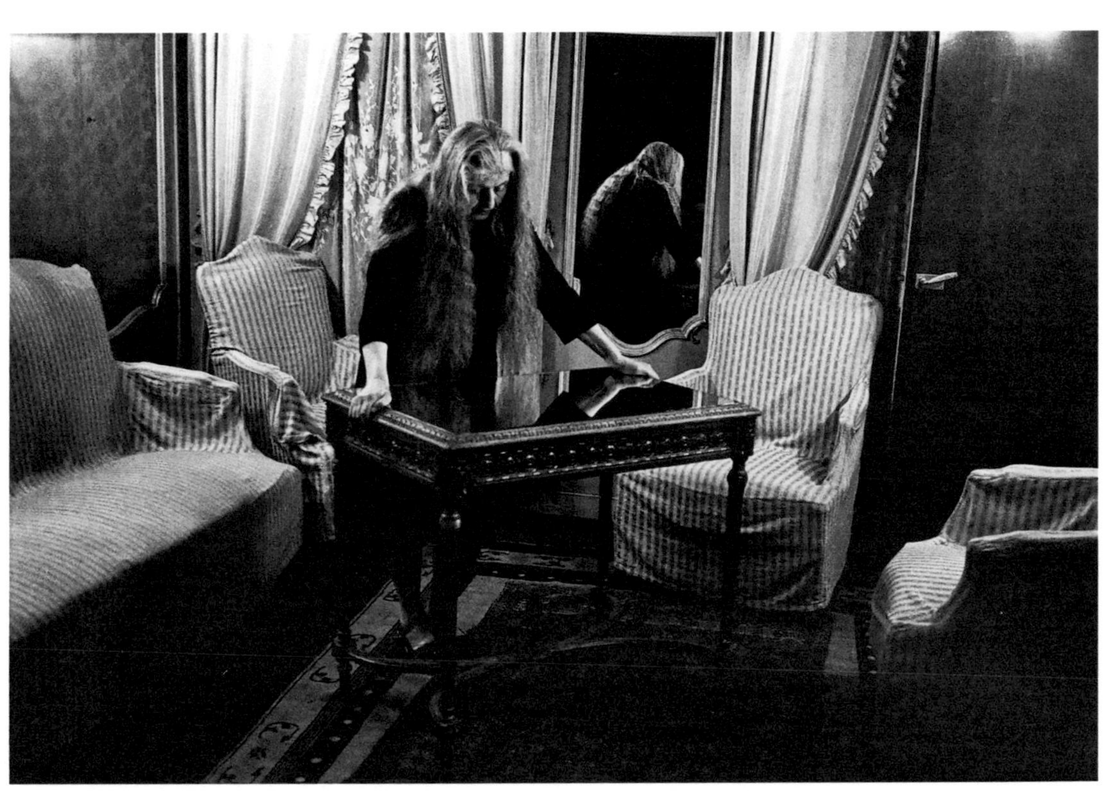

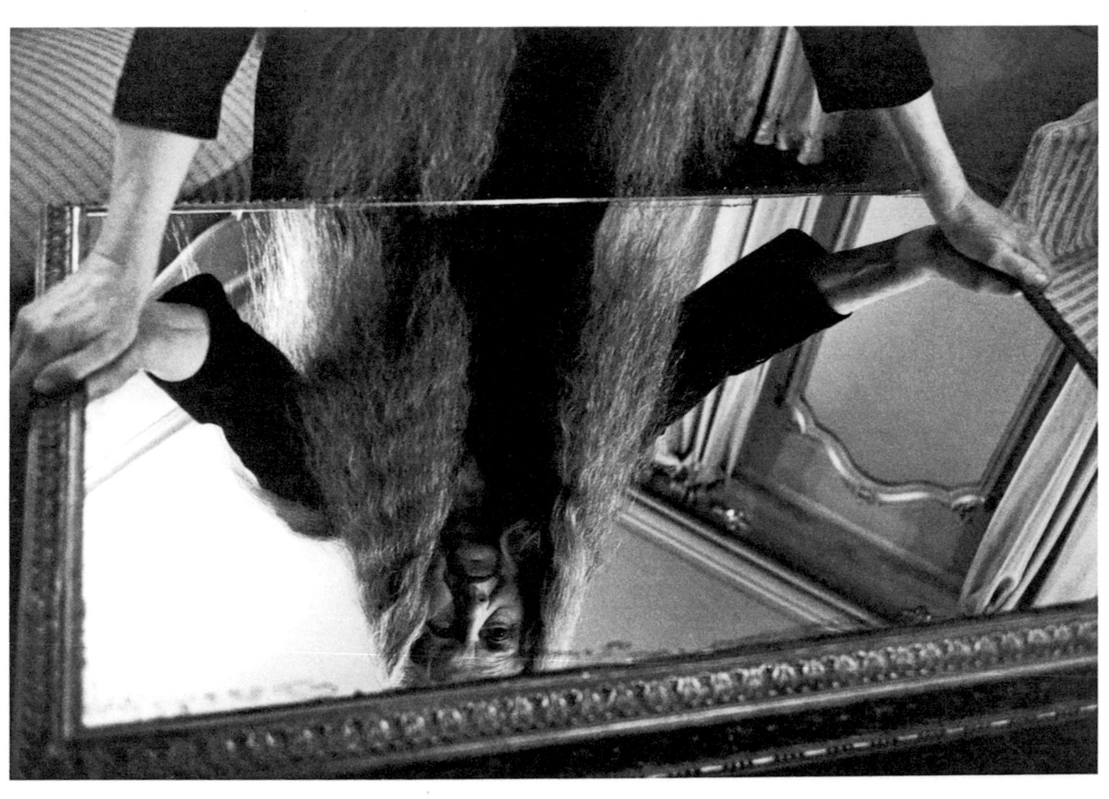

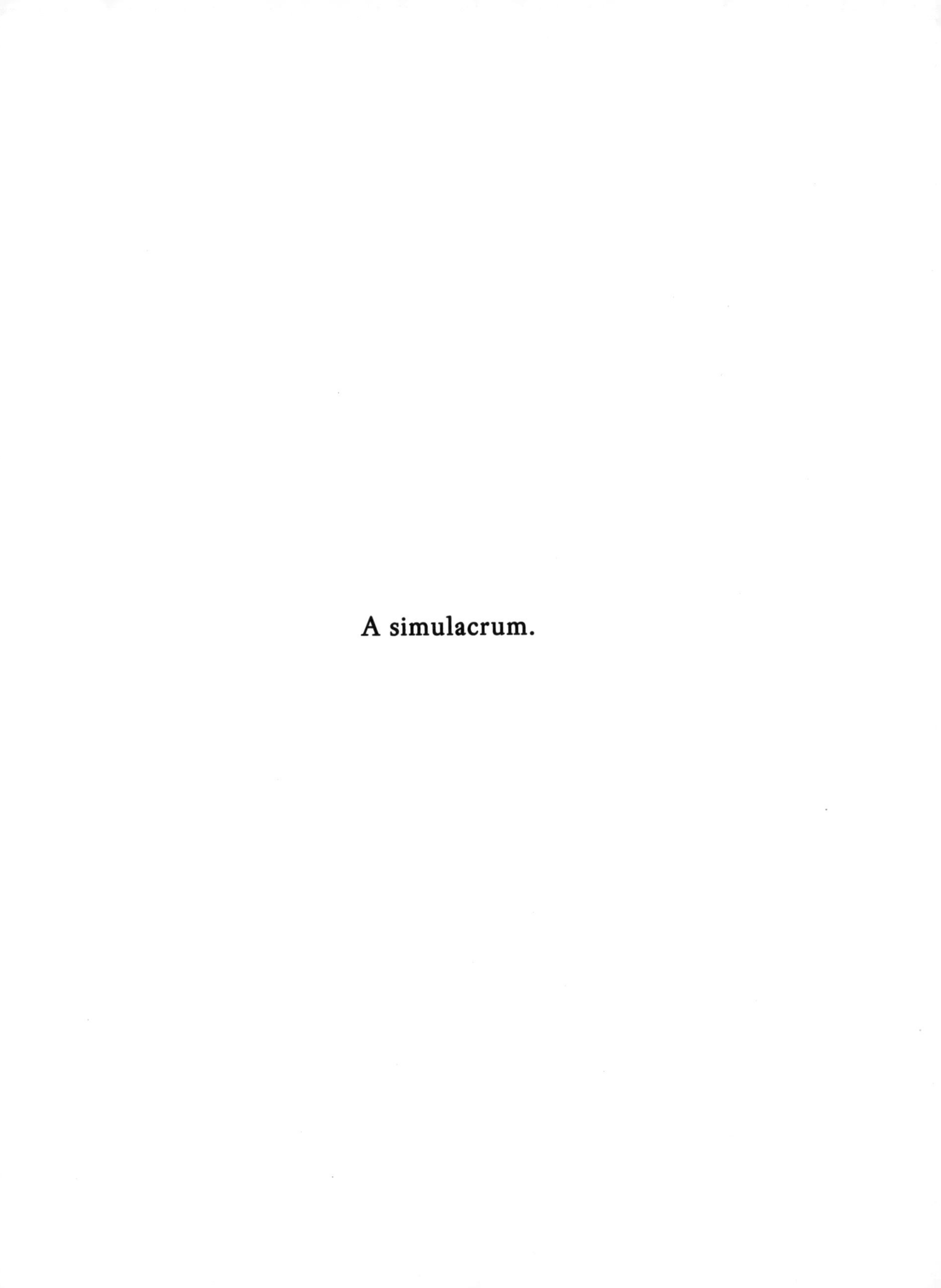

A simulacrum.

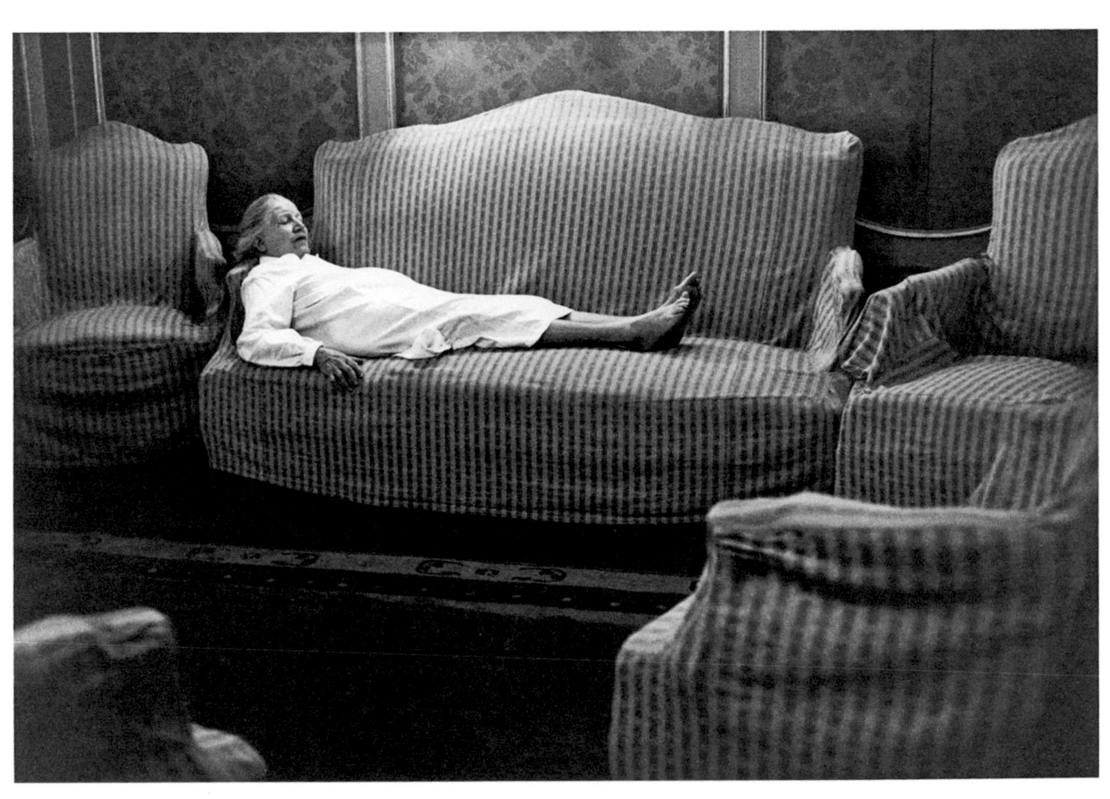

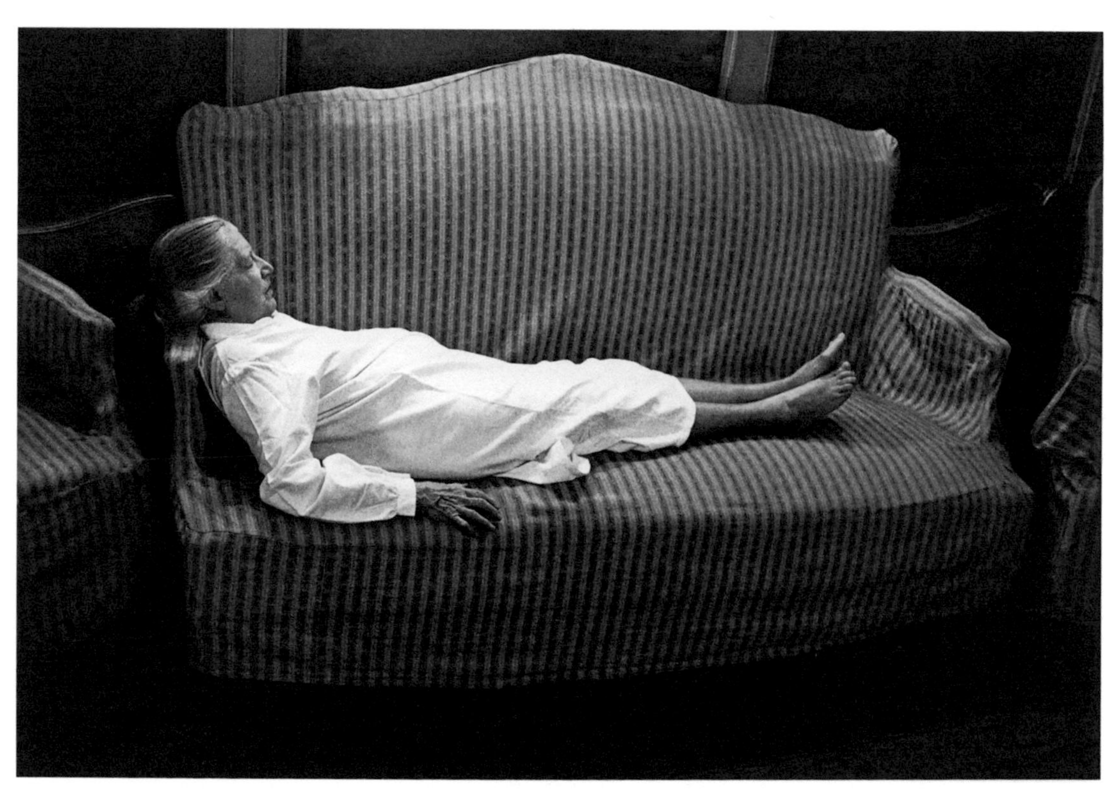

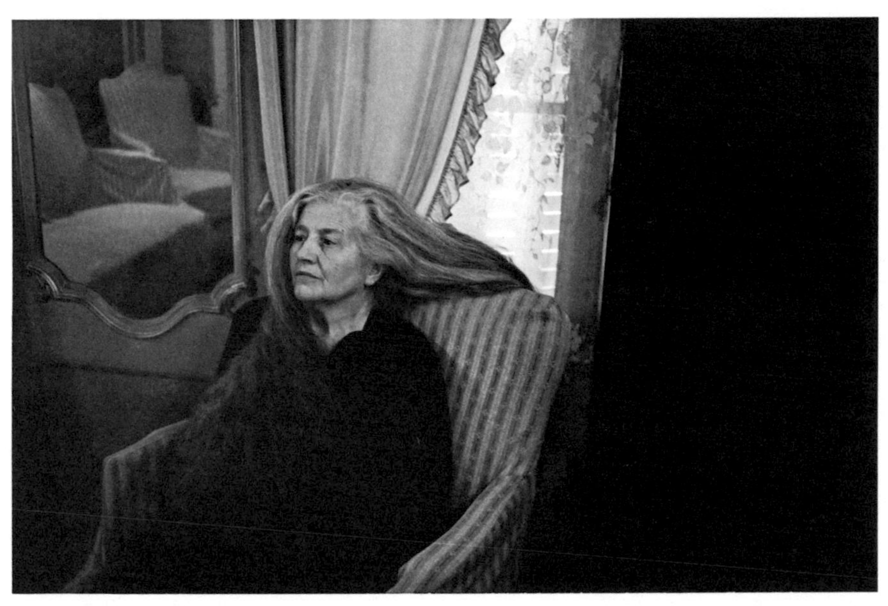

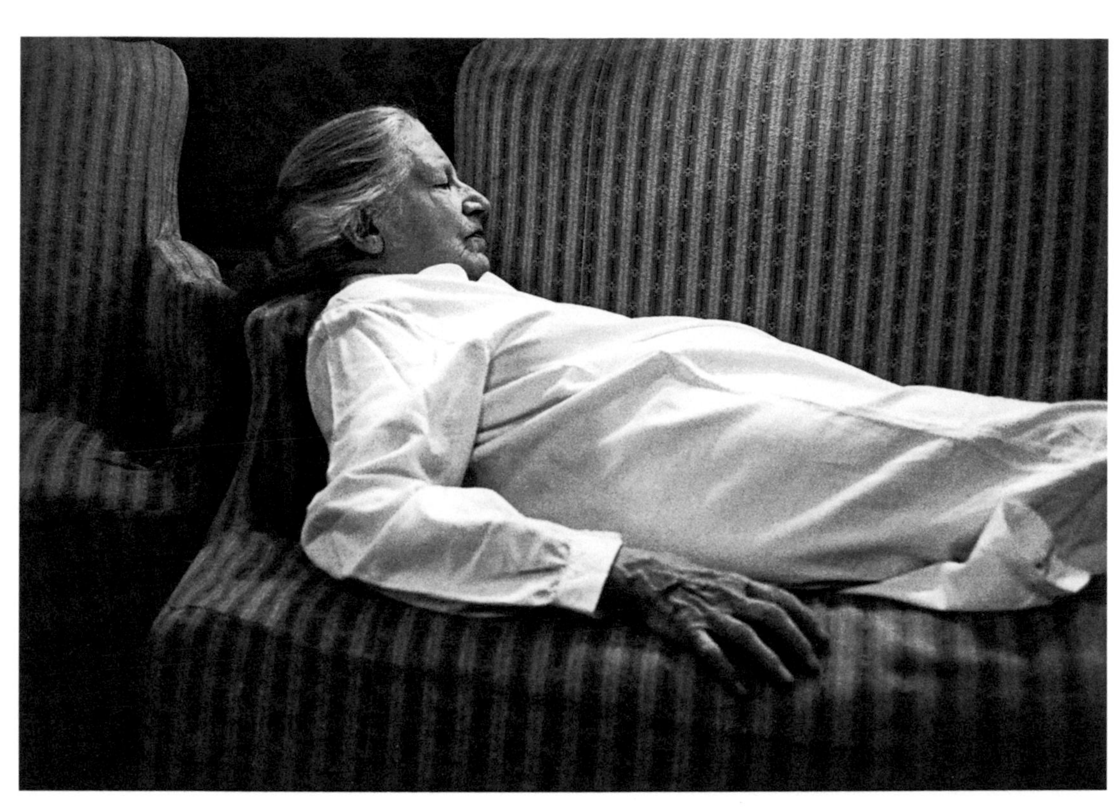

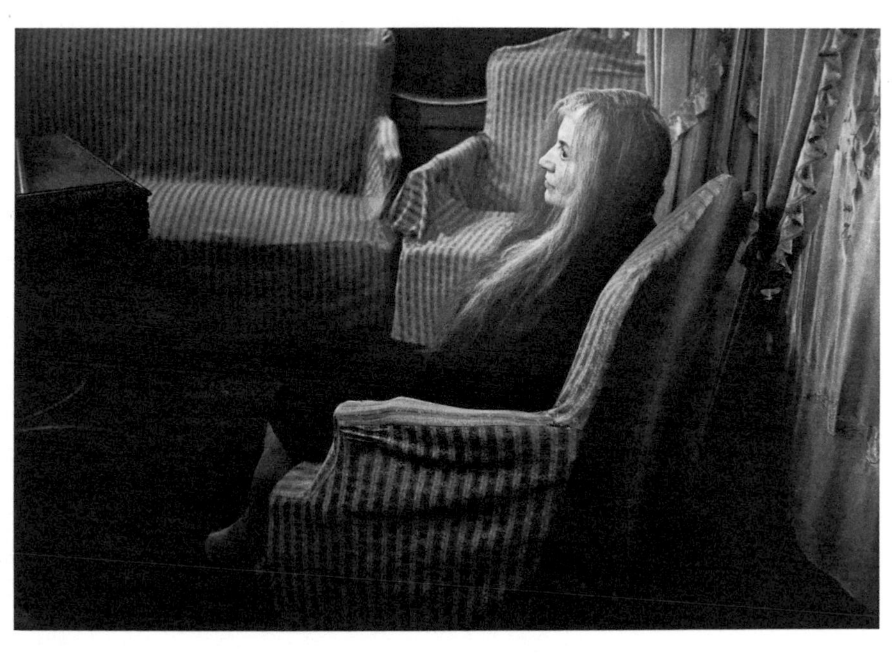

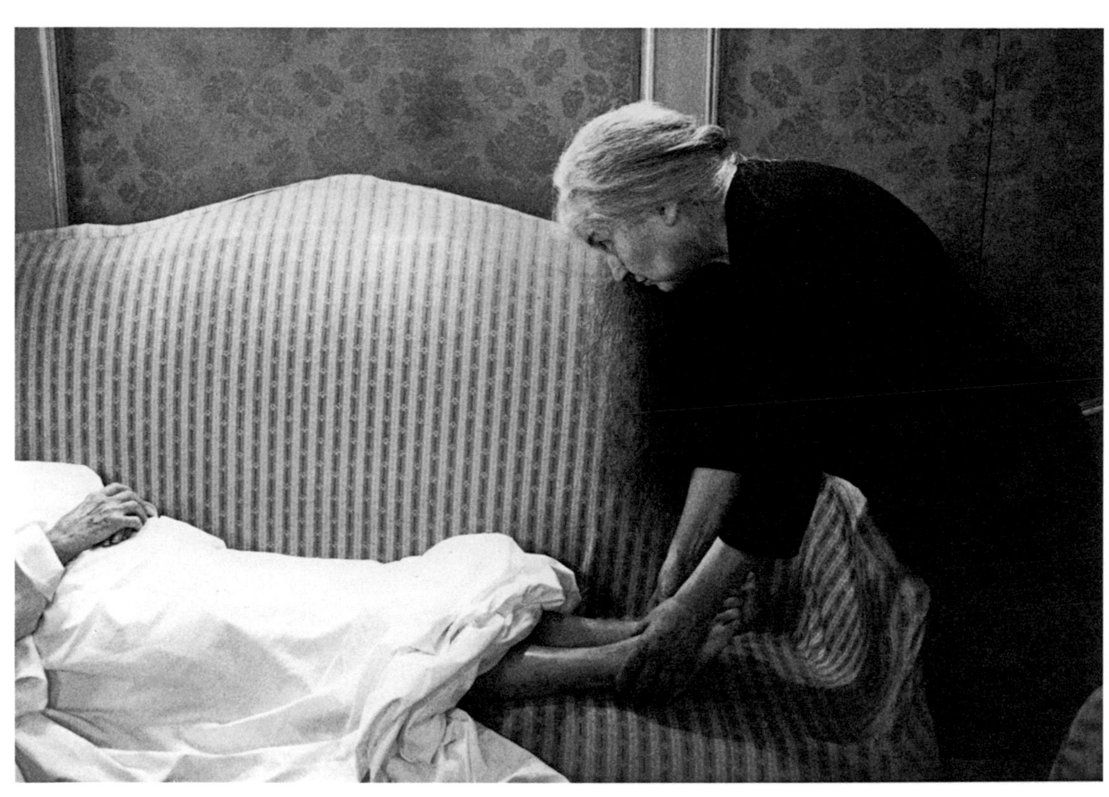

The cadaver.

Suzanne finally, almost defiantly, proposes something that speaks directly to a desire I had in our photographic relationship, one that I hadn't even dared think about before. She says to me, "Let's find the phone number for the Faculté de Medecine on their card, I want to call and ask if you can come follow my body after I die and photograph what they do with it." I then decide that I will do a series that simulates Suzanne's death, just to rid myself of the anguish that abduction will cause: as soon as she dies, the Faculté must be called, the body immediately taken away, stolen without even a wake. I learn more about what exactly happens: once taken from the van, the body is rolled up in a blanket, then placed on a trolley. It is bled over a basin from an artery cut at the base of the groin, then filled with formaldehyde through the neck. The skin turns blue very quickly, sometimes almost brown, and the entire body begins to look like wax. It is then brought down by elevator into an underground, windowless room, lit solely by neon light. A fan turns above a large vat made of transparent glass, filled with formaldehyde and floating cadavers that a man in a white shirt, standing on a ladder, stirs with a wooden pole. It smells like vinegar and disinfectant. Once the cadavers have been fully steeped, they are removed by the foot with a pulley to dry.

The body will wait in a metal drawer in a cold room until school starts, when it is given to a student. The face will be covered with a bag; fingers will only reach the body's innermost parts through the translucent membrane of a glove. No part will be preserved, but thrown one after another into a large black plastic bag, then burned.

At the end, they return to take a bow. . .

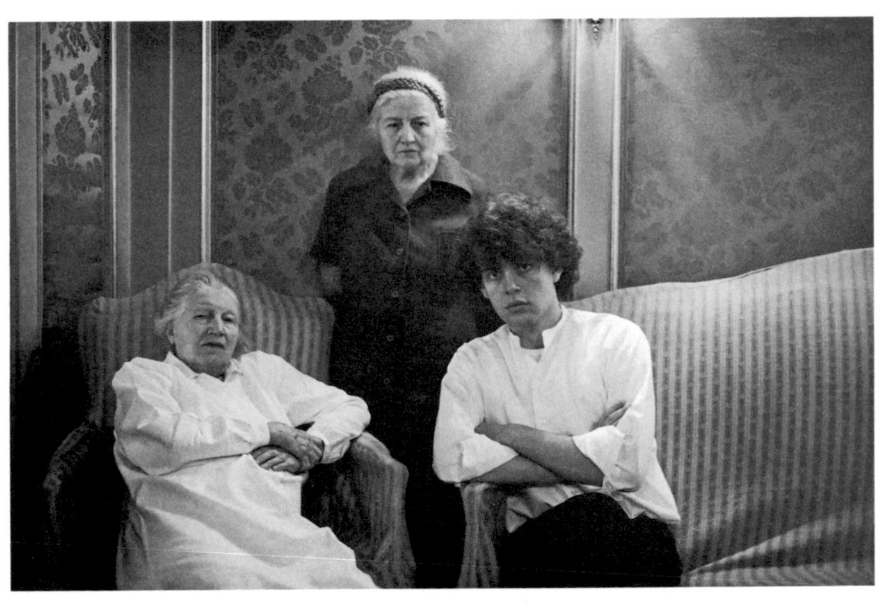

The mise-en-scene.

During the simulacrum of her death, Suzanne was a bit tense,
clinging to the edge of the sofa with her neck crammed against
the armrest, simply dressed in a white shirt. I try to improve
matters, because Louise, although there, wasn't intervening:
I make her bring a white enamel bowl with a soft, natural
sponge floating in a bit of water so that she can bathe Suzanne,
and I place a pillow under Suzanne's neck so the pose won't be
too uncomfortable, I cover her entire body with a white blanket.
Louise, barefoot, kneels at the end of the sofa. She tries to lift
the corpse by gripping it by the hands, pulling it by the feet.
They both laugh. It was an extremely hot day. For me, as I am
shooting it, the series feels like the completion, the endpoint
of the entire work. But when I look over the contact sheets,
I'm totally disappointed and don't print a single photo. I search
for the reasons for this failure with Suzanne and Louise: had
I overcomplicated the series, had I cluttered it with too many
accessories (the bowl, the white sheet) that made it seem too
forced, too obvious? The previous series, less premeditated,
and more refined, had also been more beautiful, and that's what
I'd like to keep. But Suzanne says, "I think I know why this
one's no good. First, it contains too many elements. And also,
we weren't prepared; if you had described it to us in advance,
we could have been more ready for it, more concentrated, less
reluctant." From that day on, every Saturday, I drop a text in
their mailbox, a little script in which I describe the following
day's session. I plan where I will take the photos in advance, and
ask for Suzanne and Louise, whom I refer to as characters in
my letter, to wear this or that dress, this or that pair of shoes.
I also think about if I want Louise to have her hair in braids or
hanging loose. The day after this first proposal, Louise opens

the door wearing an outfit that is exactly the opposite of
what I had asked for, and I'm not sure if I should register
my disappointment. But when I say to her, without insisting,
"Hey, you haven't put on your dark blue dress..." she
says, "No problem, I'll go and change." And she closes her
bedroom door to change her dress, and unbraid her hair...

The opening.

The day the exhibition opens, I imagine the two of them sitting
side by side on monumental thrones, their hands placed on the
ends of the armrests like queens, powdered and silent, protected
from the public, like the photos are, by a pane of glass, or by a
veil, in their best gowns, but also with their bare feet resting in
a basin half-filled with warm water that I warm up from time
to time by plunging one of those burning hot iron bars in it,
the kind they use in Switzerland to warm up beer. I'd spend the
opening doing this, in devotion to them. And their finery would
be scattered all over the walls, one of Suzanne's old dresses in
red silk edged with black lace, her gloves, some of Louise's bar-
rettes and combs, her missal, for the public to come and admire.

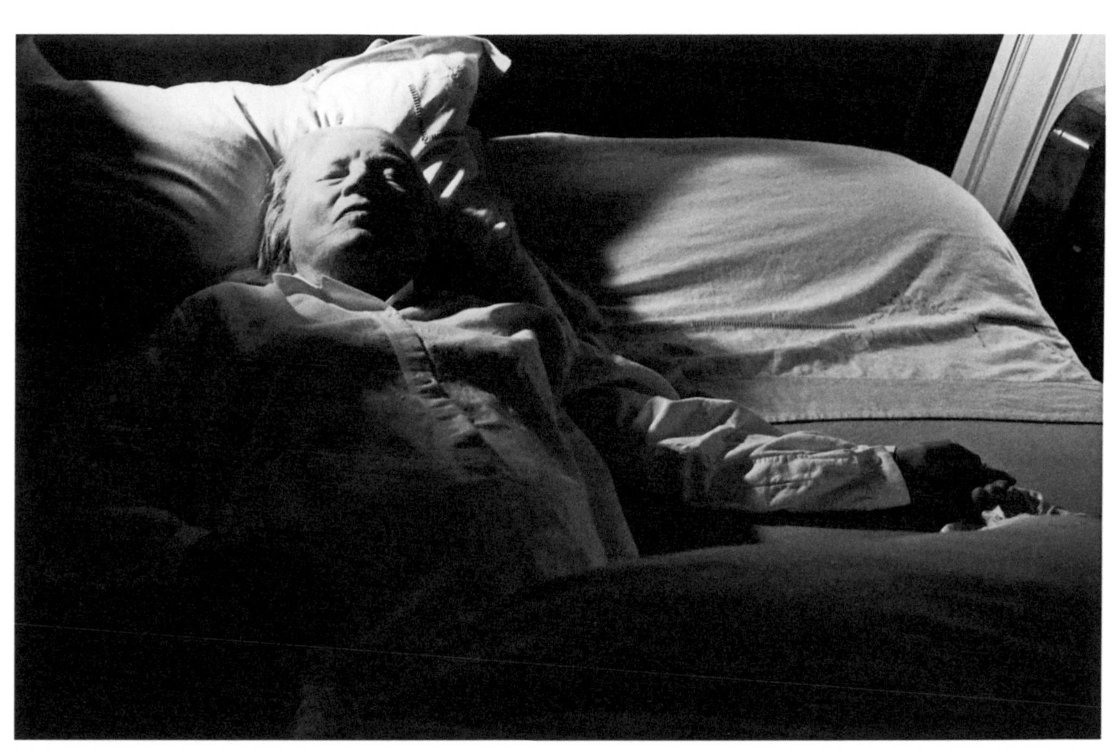

The screenplay.

Louise finally comes to see the exhibition with my mother. She wears a headscarf to hide her braids, for fear that someone might recognize her. I'm sort of nervous, since she hasn't ever read the texts before. The next day, in front of Suzanne, sick and in bed, my mother tells me that Louise burst out laughing while reading them. Suzanne, with a bit of sadness for the irony of it, says, "I guess I didn't need to hide that letter... you read it to the whole world..." Louise comes into the bedroom and says, "Bravo, bravo on your exhibition! Oh, some of those photos are really stunning. That one where you're dead, Suzanne, it's really very good!" And she begins to tell Suzanne, enthusiastically (while I sit there, practically mortified) the story of the vat of formaldehyde and the hook...

Suzanne and Louise get "their picture in the papers." Articles begin to appear about the exhibit which I bring them as they come out, and they comment on them, they think they're good, more or less. I meet Louise on the street, who tells me, "Look, they're beginning to talk about us a little bit too much." When an article appears in *Cinematographer* in which a "passion for old women" is associated with the "opposite of pedophilia," Suzanne calls me outraged to say, "So, if I'm understanding it correctly, he's speaking squarely of incest... and then, 'pedophile,' what does that mean? I looked it up in the dictionary, it doesn't even exist!" I say, "You must have some old dictionaries..."

Finally, one Sunday, at lunch, I talk to them again about the film, since for me, rekindling the idea of a project with them gives me a reason to live, and defies death a little bit. "There was the play, there was the photo novel, now I would like to make a film with you." They don't say no. Louise says, "We'll have to wait a while before my hair grows back." And Suzanne: "And I'll have to sleep a lot if I'm going to be ready for your film." I write the screenplay in two days, since it had been running through my head for a while. And the day I bring it to my producer, my approach really makes me feel as if I were my aunts' manager...

Scene 49. Exterior, day.

Two men in workers' uniforms cross the garden, carrying on their backs, in their arms, Suzanne's wooden bedposts, paintings wrapped up in newspaper, the two Chinese lamps...

Scene 50. Interior, day.

We first see, through the kitchen window, the dead pigeon, half-decomposed, on the roof of the garage. Louise, in the kitchen, places her chair in front of the window and sits down on it. We watch her like this for some time, her back, while on the soundtrack, noises from the outside world emerge, growing with greater and greater intensity. And so, at first muffled and then dissolving over time, floating in silence:

– television noise (constant interruptions)
– a baby who begins to cry and suddenly stops
– birdsong
– a man singing, imitating a tenor
– barking
– an ambulance siren
– a Spanish man grabbing a woman (a domestic dispute)
– continuous radio noise
– a woman sneezing
– a great burst of brief, collective laughter
– a man concluding an unintelligible story, followed by applause
– TV show theme songs
– children at play
– a scream of horror, sharp, from a woman in a film on television . . .

The final credits roll, transparently projected over the image
of Louise seated at the window, and over the first movement
of Franck's sonata for violin and piano, which replaces
the noise, and which is Suzanne's favorite piece of music.

Hervé Guibert
January, 1980.

Translator's Notes

1   Another slip of the tongue: there are in
fact fourteen stations of the cross, not forty.

2   A medieval French term, to denote
chain-mail stockings worn by knights
of the era. Civilians also wore a woolen
version as leggings.

The Making of Suzanne and Louise
Thomas Simonnet

Suzanne and Louise, the second book published by Hervé Guibert, appeared in 1980, three years after *Propaganda Death*. In a radio interview, recorded in 1980, he describes the genesis of *Suzanne and Louise* in detail.[1] "My first idea, six years ago, had been to make a film about them." But his great-aunts—his maternal grandmother's sisters—categorically refused. He abandoned the screenplay.

He then decides to write a play that was "something like the failed film I couldn't make." Entitled *Louise and Suzanne*, he reads it at the Gueuloir à Avignon festival and recounts the experience in his first article published in *Le Monde*.[2] He records a reading by Michael Lonsdale and Michel Foucault. The play is never produced.

In 1978, Hervé Guibert returns to his initial film project. He intends to shoot it after his great-aunts' deaths —with "actresses who will play their roles, in their house, with their belongings and their clothes." With this in mind, he photographs them every Sunday, "piling up" the contact sheets without printing the photographs— traces, proofs of their existence that he hopes to reflect in his film to come.

After six months, he finally prints some photos and shows them to Suzanne and Louise, who, he says, are "surprised by the images I gave back to them." They then agree to participate in the project and, every Saturday, he delivers "a little script that describes the following day's session" to their mailbox.

In 1979, Guibert exhibits photographs of his great-aunts at the Remise du Parc in Paris, along with photos of the wax

1   Radio interview with Gérard-Julien Salvy, "Demarche," broadcast on France Culture, July 5, 1980.
2   "Un auteur en quête de spectateur," *Le Monde*, August 17, 1977, reprinted in Hervé Guibert, *Articles Intrépides*, Gallimard, 2008.

Hervé Guibert

SUZANNE ET LOUISE

(Film)

Hervé GUIBERT

"LOUISE ET SUZANNE"

(Dialogues)

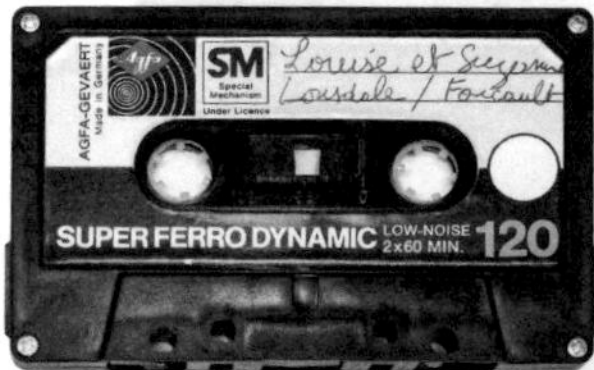

Suzanne et Louise
Film.

Prégénérique : voix off (texte du prologue) sur carton noir 9 "Tous les
Générique : lettres blanches sur carton noir.   dimanche, depuis l'enfance, j'allais
déjeuner chez mes grand-tantes, Suzanne
et Louise —

1) C'est le matin, le réveil, sept heures du matin, au début de l'été.
Le film (le prégénérique) commence par une série de plans-photos qui
montrent le lieu où vit Louise, ses objets, la marque de sa présence,
sans la montrer elle-même. Ainsi :

. Son grand lit ouvert, avec la petite croix de bois noir qui le
surplombe, et dans les plissures du drap, dont on voit aussi
les initiales (L.J.) brodées, l'empreinte du corps qui vient de
le quitter, et le poste de radio éteint posé aussi sur le drap,
à côté.

. La sorte de petit autel qui fait face au lit de Louise, installé
sur un buffet : la statue en plâtre du Christ, une vierge,
des rameaux de buis, des vases et deux photos de Suzanne et
de Louise jeunes, encadrées.

. Cette reproduction en noir et blanc du Christ de Vélasquez
qui est accrochée au-dessus de la porte.

. Les chaussures alignées de Louise dans le couloir.

Puis on voit, prise depuis une fenêtre du troisième étage, la
fenêtre de la salle de bain du 2ème étage, et Louise, en chemise
de nuit, qui y passe rapidement.

2) Le jardin touffu de l'été, en bas de l'hôtel particulier.
Louise, qu'on voit d'abord de dos, en tablier, et qui porte un
grand cabas noir pousse la porte du jardin et s'en va.

2.

DECOR.

Un hôtel particulier en démolition. Les fenêtres sont des
trous qui donnent sur le ciel. Toute la façade a été arrachée.
Les plafonds sont défoncés. Au premier étage: les restes
luxueux d'un appartement Louis XVI, un lit, un tableau, un
lustre de perles. Reliée à cet appartement par une passerelle:
une baignoire. Au deuxième étage: les éléments d'une cuisine,
table de bois simple, pendule et poste de radio. Dans la
pièce d'à côté: une chambre qui révèle une existence
ascétique, un lit surmonté d'une croix, une armoire presque
pendue dans le vide. Tout le troisième étage s'est effondré
et s'amoncelle sous forme de débris au rez-de-chaussée. Ce
qui reste d'un escalier relie les deux étages.

PERSONNAGES.

- SUZANNE, quatre-vingt ans, vit au premier étage.
- LOUISE, sa soeur, soixante-dix ans, vit au deuxième étage
  avec Whysky, un gros berger allemand.
(Ces deux rôles pourront être tenus par de jeunes actrices).

Cassette tape of the recording of *Louise et Suzanne*
by Michael Londsdale and Michel Foucault.
The original typescripts and manuscript of *Suzanne and Louise* (film)
and *Louise and Suzanne* (dialogue).

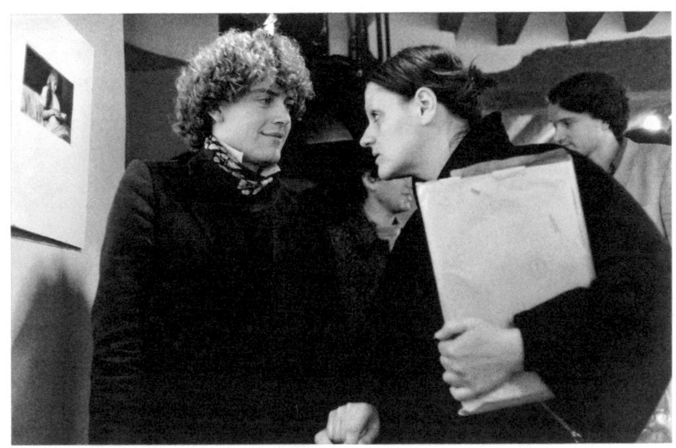

Above: Hervé Guibert and Zouc at the opening
of his exhibition at Agathe Gaillard gallery, 1980
Following pages: Two contact sheets, 1978

sculptures at the Musée Grévin.[3] It's the first time that he shows his work to the public. "Hervé came to see all of the exhibits at the gallery," remembers Samia Saouma, the gallery's director. "We became friends and would have dinner together once a month. He told me about his mysterious and slightly disturbing aunts… I was thrilled to offer him that show. Our conversations were less about photography and more about life, his writer friends and close friends."[4] One critic, in *Cinématographe*, describes the atmosphere perfectly: "When one enters 'la Remise du Parc,' one is at first surprised by the small scale of the works presented: none of the works are larger than a postcard, and all are surrounded by large mats that make them seem even smaller. The prints are very black, cold, almost hard. The gallery itself, at the end of a long hallway painted white, contributes to this austere feeling. […] Along the wall, an alternation between photographs and texts, arranged by an internal order —these are only "snatches" of a novel, apparently yet to be written. […] A series of three or four photographs follows a section of text, without that text necessarily commenting on those photos."[5]

It's only after that exhibit that Hervé Guibert pursues the publication of a "photo novel" about Suzanne and

3   "Les coulisses du Musée Grevin, and Suzanne and Louise, bribes" was held from October 24 to November 24, 1979. The gallery was located at 2, impasse des Bourdonnais, in the 1st arrondissement.
4   Interview conducted on December 19, 2018.

5   "Suzanne and Louise," Pierre Jouvet, *Cinématographe* n°52, November 1979.

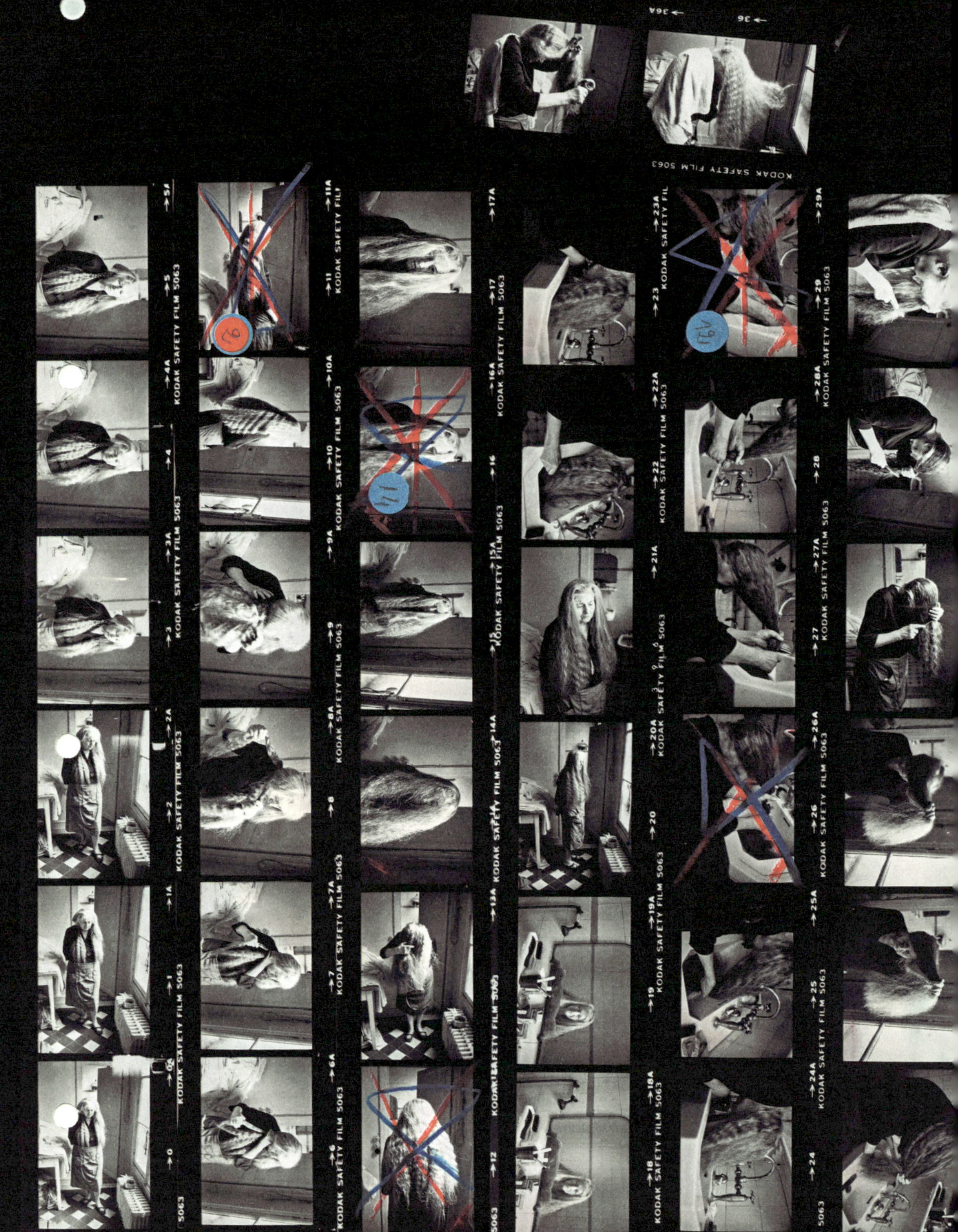

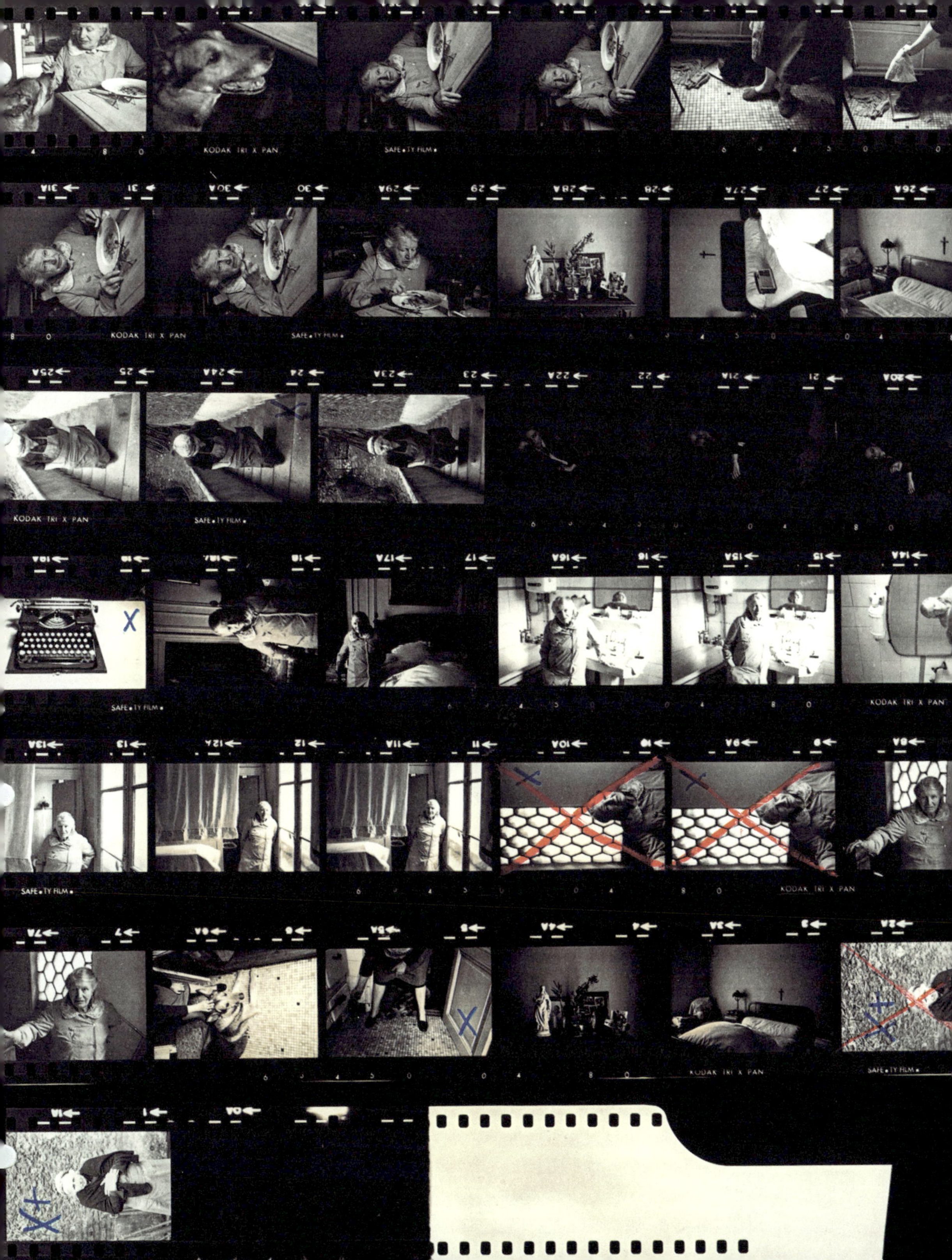

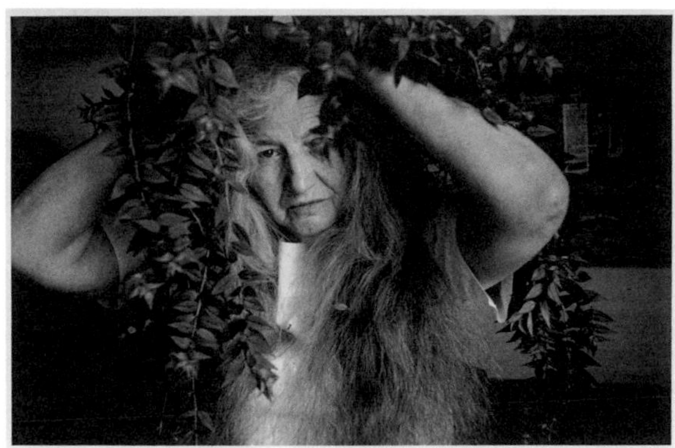

Louise. For the text, he drew from his screenplay, his play, and the notes that he took in his journal after every work session with his great-aunts in order, he said, to "dub" the photographs and "to note their reactions."[6] Photographer Jean-Philippe Charbonnier advised him to preserve his written manuscript.[7]

Jean-Luc Hennig, writer and journalist at *Libération*, had written a very favorable review of *Propaganda Death* and had received a warm reply in return from Guibert, but had never met him. "When I launched the 'Illustrations' series at Éditions Libres Hallier, under the auspices of Albin Michel, I contacted him and immediately offered to publish him. He came to see me at the newspaper and proposed a 'photo novel.' Sight unseen, I agreed to the idea. I didn't interfere in the book. I let him do exactly what he wanted. I love that book: no narration, fragmented, shattered into dust. Every photo is self-sufficient."[8]

The layout, which Guibert wrote in his own handwriting on the back of the photo itself, was used directly by the printer during the book's production. Carefully preserved by the author in his archives, it demonstrates the keen sense of the book and its *mise en page*.[9]

When the book was printed in April, 1980, Agathe Gaillard had been running a gallery exclusively dedicated to photography since 1975. Guibert,

6   Radio interview, ibid.
7   Manuscript of *Suzanne and Louise* dedicated to Jean-Phillipe Charbonnier by Hervé Guibert, Coll. Agathe Gaillard.

8   Interview conducted December 19, 2018.
9   The remarkable conservation of this layout made this current edition possible.

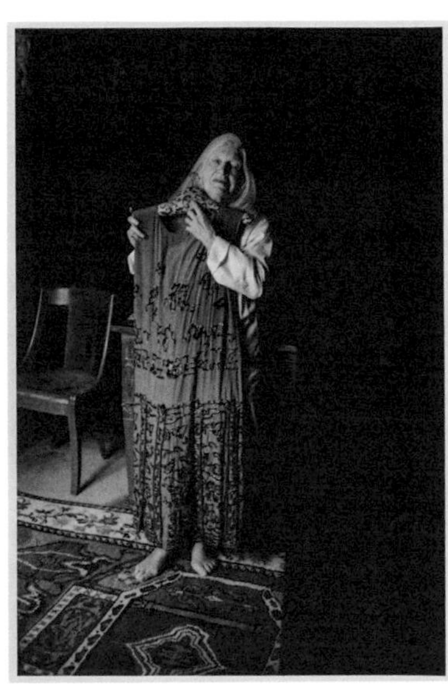

Suzanne (left) and Louise (above) preparing for their sessions.
Unpublished prints, not selected by Hervé Guibert.

a photo critic at *Le Monde* since 1977, had been a frequent visitor: "Hervé played a tremendous role in the promotion of photography. He saw it as a form of *écriture* and got it accepted. It's interesting to note that writers were, at the time, the first ones to support photography: Hervé, Roland Barthes, Denis Roche…"[10] Agathe Gaillard was very familiar with Guibert's photography work, but "to show a critic would have been shocking." She hesitates, until the release of *Suzanne and Louise* decides for her. For three weeks, from May 4–24, 1980, the exhibition of the photographs from the book is very well received, and "Hervé and his guests make the opening a success." Soon after, she brings a signed copy to the photographer André Kertész, who is "charmed and delighted by its elegant impropriety."[11]

After 1980, Suzanne and Louise regularly appear in Guibert's work. First in his photography, as is demonstrated by the new portraits that appear in the 1984 show at Galerie Agathe Gaillard, "Le seul visage." Then in a 1988 novel, in which they are the principal characters: *The Gangsters*, published by Éditions de Minuit. Then again in his only film, *Modesty, or Immodesty* (1991), which includes several sequences of him talking with his great-aunts. And he invokes them regularly in his journal, *The Mausoleum of Lovers* (published posthumously in 2001).

He repeats the use of handwritten script in his *L'Autre Journal* between

10   Interview conducted December 20, 2018.

11   Agathe Gaillard, *Mémoires d'une galerie*, coll. "Témoins de l'art," Gallimard, 2013, p. 41.

1985 and 1986, in captions that describe and reflect upon the book's photographic portraits.[12] Certain locations and themes in the photographs of *Suzanne and Louise* have a long-standing history in his photographic oeuvre. Bedrooms, bathrooms, corridors, little altars of objects, tables, mirrors, curtains, divans, more handwriting, recumbent figures, readers…

Hervé Guibert pursued an ongoing inquiry into the relationship between image and text. Each of the two books he produced that include photos takes a different slant. Where *Suzanne and Louise*, in 1980, juxtaposed text and image, *Le seul visage*, published by Minuit in 1984, presents only photographs, but hijacks the layout usually used for novels at Éditions de Minuit. For *Vice* in 1991, the short texts that compose the book are very clearly separated from the nineteen photographs that compose a separate section.[13] Printed on a different kind of paper, they are designed to be one step of a "journey."

In a span of fifteen years, Suzanne and Louise, at first so unwilling in their grand-nephew's project, become essential accomplices to his work. With tenderness and a touch of irony, Suzanne dedicates in her own handwriting a copy of *Suzanne and Louise*: "To our very dear 'grand-nephew' Hervé, in admiration for having pulled from our obscurity this book, which is too brilliant for our modesty."

Suzanne died at 95 on January 16, 1991, the same year as Hervé Guibert, with Louise following several years later. At 14, rue François Villon, on the site of their *hôtel particulier*, there now stands a modern apartment building.

---

12 See Hervé Guibert, *L'Autre Journal*, Gallimard, 2015.

13 Hervé Guibert, *Vice*, Jacques Bertoin, 1991, reprinted by Gallimard, 2013.

SOURIRE   6

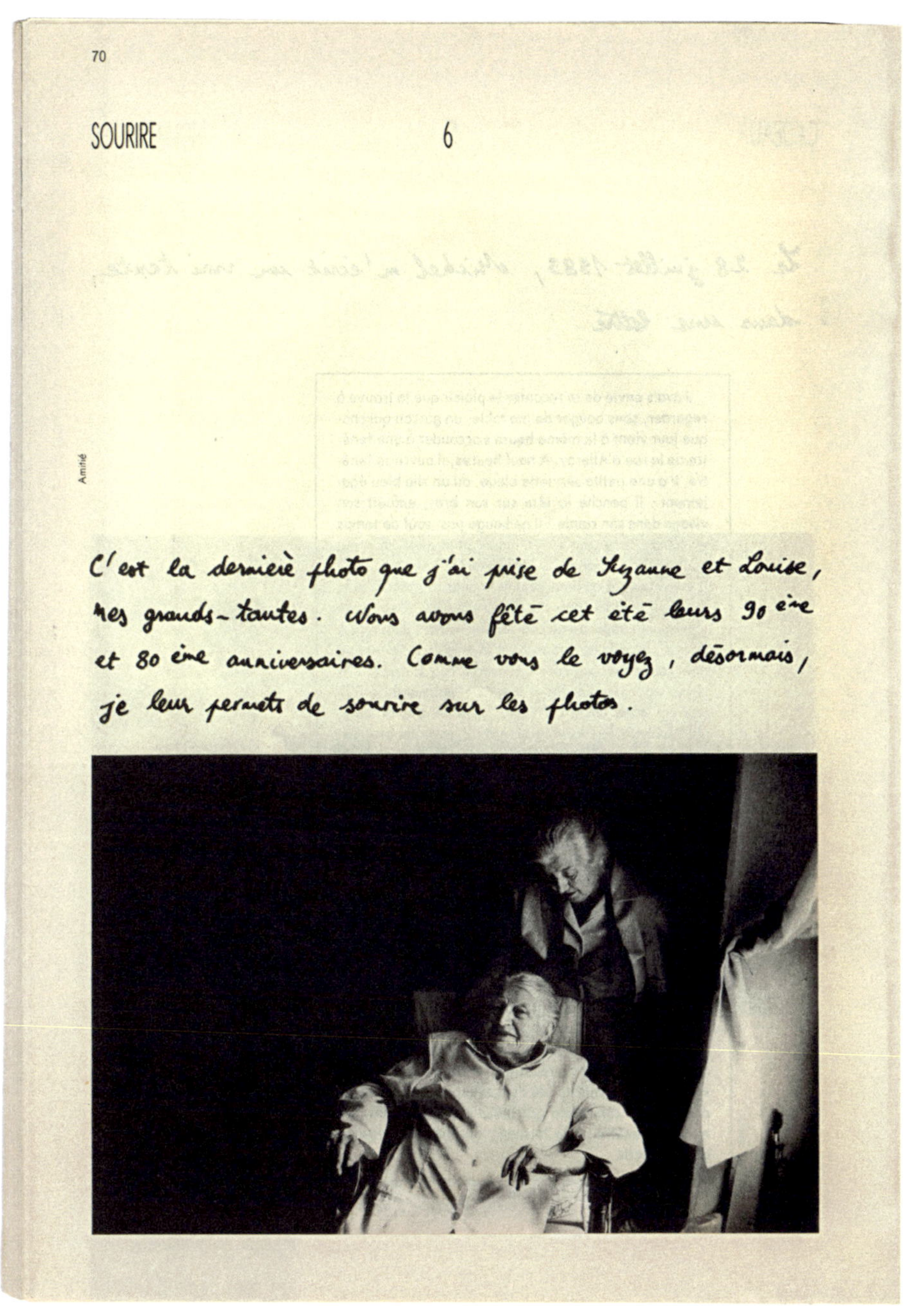

Above: Suzanne and Louise in *L'Autre Journal*, 1985
Next page: Spreads from the 2019 edition of *Suzanne and Louise*
published by L'arbalète/Gallimard, Gallimard

La photo.

Je crois que ce sont d'autres choses, que des objectifs, qui font les "bonnes photos", des choses immatérielles, de l'ordre de l'amour, ou de l'âme, des forces qui passent là et qui s'inscrivent, funestes, comme le texte qui se fait malgré soi, dicté par une voix supérieure…

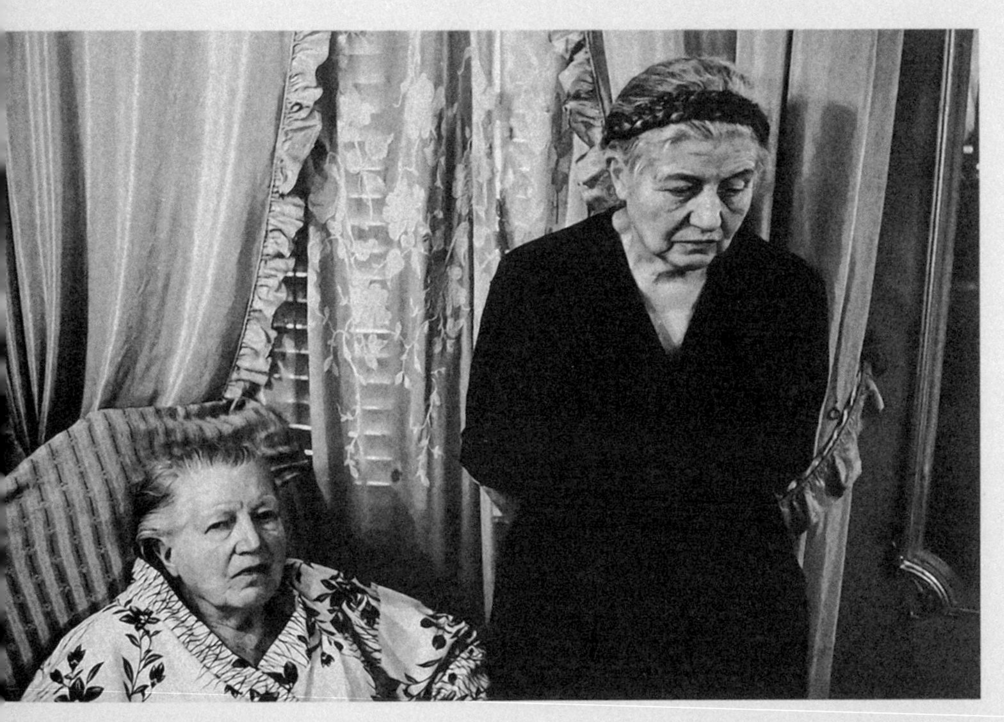

PUBLISHER'S ACKNOWLEDGEMENTS

Thank you to Philo Cohen for paving the
way of this book from French to its English
translation, for her collaboration and for
her instrumental enthusiasm in bringing
this book to life.

Thank you to Moyra Davey for not only
writing the introduction, but for introducing
me to the book and for being involved in
every aspect of the making of this edition.

Thank you to Christine Pichini for her
meticulous care in translating Guibert's
particular and idiosyncratic text.

Thank you to Nicolas Linnert for his
sensitivity in his edit of the text and
for his dedication to this book.

Thank you to Santiago da Silva and his
studio for their light touch and sophisticated
eyes in all design aspects of this book.

Special thanks to:
Matt Connors, Benoît Demaria, Ben Estes,
Alex Foxton, Louis Fratino, Jason Fulford,
Craig Garrett, Nan Goldin, Jérôme Gris,
Christine Guibert, Dina Khalil, Wayne
Koestenbaum, Josh Lawson, Julie Le Men,
Matt Litvack, Duane Michals, Margot Miriel,
Maggie Nelson, Francis Schichtel, Jason
Simon, Rachel Valinsky, Adam Weitzman

– Jordan Weitzman, Magic Hour Press